ALSO BY IRENE J. DUMAS

A Salute to Our Veterans
Vignettes of Those Who Made the Difference
1939-2000

A Salute to Our Veterans
Vignettes of the "Can Do" Navy Seabees
1942-2007

Veterans and Still Rollin'
Pip Printing, Burlington, NJ
Copyright 2003

A SALUTE
TO OUR
VETERANS

*Vignettes of Those Who Served Side-by-Side
For our American Freedom—1918-2007*

IRENE J. DUMAS

Order this book online at www.trafford.com
or email orders@trafford.com

Most Trafford titles are also available at major online book retailers.

Printed in the United States of America.

ISBN: 978-1-4907-1647-3 (sc)
ISBN: 978-1-4907-1649-7 (hc)
ISBN: 978-1-4907-1648-0 (e)

Library of Congress Control Number: 2013918277

Trafford rev. 10/29/2013

www.trafford.com
North America & international
toll-free: 1 888 232 4444 (USA & Canada)
fax: 812 355 4082

For my son Danny, a true patriot,

December 31, 1962-April 18, 2003

With love to my very supportive and patient husband, Lt. Kenneth
Douglas Gammon, my precious daughter Renee, encouraging
and loving sons, William, Timothy and Robert and my dear
sisters, Alberta (Bert), Anne(Tiny) and Christine (Chris).

Factual accounts by the veterans in my book went into the writing
of it. However, I accept sole responsibility for its contents.

Irene J. Dumas-Gammon

Waverly-Lakeland, Florida

September 2013

INTRODUCTION

A SALUTE TO OUR VETERANS

This book has been written for the men and women that served for our country during World War One, World War Two, the Korean War, the Vietnam War, and the Gulf War. They also served during the Cuban Crisis, Grenada Crisis, Desert Storm and Desert Shield, in Lebanon, Afghanistan and the Iraq War, etc.

The Veterans that are featured in this book gave to our country that part of their lives that was so powerful, knowing that when they entered into the United States military that they would most likely be sent to another country, away from their homeland, away from their families and friends, away from the place that they had grown up and had been taught how to read and write, away to a place where the people didn't speak the same language that they knew. In fact, away from all that they were and knew before their military service.

Moreover, if you think about it long enough or for one moment, one instant, one twinkle, or one second, and we considered that the Allied Forces of World War One had lost the war! What if we as Americans, English, Canadians, etc. had to give up our right to Freedom, because we had to cease fire, withdraw, throw in the towel, relinquish, renounce, show or wave a white flag? What if we had to surrender to the enemy?

I have often pondered about it and tried visioning myself in a place where I may possibly be if the reverse had happened, if the United States had to surrender during World War One or World War Two, if the enemy had occupied our country, many things can happen and many things did happen to other countries.

The veterans in this book also served in the United States military to fight for our country, like our fore-fathers did, they did it for their families, they did it for their friends and neighbors, they did it for politicians and our religious leaders, and they did it to keep the American flag waving; and they fought so that our country could remain free.

The Veterans featured in this book served honorably, courageously, willingly, righteously, and nobly and without any regrets. That is why I feel that their military history should be documented and forever remain in the Liberty of Congress and local libraries, so that future generations are able to research back and reflect on these brave United States Veterans.

I have listed the Veterans in this book according to dates that they served, the earliest being those veterans that served during World War Two and so on.

I have also reserved the last chapter of this book for Veterans that served in the Military and are no longer with us; they are veterans of families and friends that you and I have known perhaps before their passing. Fortunately, their families and friends have not forgotten them and their military history service, and therefore; I am proud to have been able to include them in this book. I pray you enjoy reading about the life and duty among these veterans as much as I enjoyed learning about them.

Irene J. Dumas-Gammon

TABLE OF CONTENTS

A SALUTE TO OUR VETERANS

Vignettes of Those Who Served Side-by Side

For Our American Freedom

1918-2007

World War One—It is well known in the American History books that during World War One, long before the Americans entered into that war, that the German-Foreign Minister, while his country was at peace with the United States, had urged the German Minister in Mexico to arrange for a Mexican Invasion of the United States promising to Mexico a slice of the American territory.

Also, after the Germans sunk the Lusitania, murdered Nurse Cavell and converted Northern France into a wilderness of death and destruction; the American people started to take notice. Officially during that time, United States was neutral, and the United States President Woodrow Wilson had sent several exchanges of notes to Germany, the last one closed with a declaration that if Germany violated the rights of the U.S. upon the high seas, the United States, would hold her at "strict accountability".

Following President Wilson's last note, the last day of January 1917 Germany announced to the world that she would wage war on the sea with unrestricted frightfulness. Thus she repudiated her pledges to the U.S., and intimated that she would torpedo without warning every ship that dared to sail the seas.

On 2nd April 1917 President Wilson went before congress and asked that diplomatic relations with Germany be severed, his last hope that the United States would be able to maintain armed neutrality, soon vanished.

The Senate passed the war declaration on 4 April by a vote of 82 to 6, and the House of Representatives passed the vote on 6 April by 373 to 50 votes. Twenty-two days after the declaration of War, Congress passed conscription of our law providing for the selective draft.

In a few weeks the regular Army, by volunteering was brought up to strength of 287,000 troops and the National Guard up to 625,000 troops. On 5 June ten million young Americans registered and became available, when required for the purposes of National cause.

The Allies also made the most urgent representations of the U.S. to speed up the transportation of troops in Europe. It was found that the United States was making preparations for war in 1919-1920 and was far behind in its program for providing airplanes, guns and munitions in 1918.

The American Army was without adequate divisional organization for the troops when they landed in France and the training of the troops could not be hurriedly completed on the continent. The Allies, however, persuaded the U.S. to rush forward troops without full equipment promising to make up all deficiencies, themselves.

General Pershing, cooperated by submitting trained American troops to be brigaded for service with British and French troops. The American troops would go forward at the rate of 250,000 a month.

By the end of June, General Pershing who was appointed to the Chief Command of the United States Expeditionary Forces and the first contingent of American troops were safe on the soil of France.

From then on there was no stopping the American Soldier, the United States men fought along and with the Allies; the British, French, Italians, Russians, Belgium's, Serbians and the Rumanians. They fought at Chateau-Thierry, St. Mihiel, the Argonne Forest, the Mossell River, Metz, the

Woevie Forest, Port-surf-seille, etc. It was a horrific price paid in blood, tears and money to save our civilization and freedom.

World War Two—While the Japanese diplomats talked peace in Washington, the Japanese torpedo bombers struck at Pearl Harbor on Sunday morning, 7 December 1941. The USS Arizona Battleship was completely loss while nineteen other ships there were wrecked or damaged (including eight battleships). One hundred-seventy-seven planes destroyed, three thousand-three-hundred-three, service men killed or missing, and one thousand-two-hundred-twenty-seven wounded. On Monday, 8 December 1941 President Roosevelt appeared before Congress at noon to deliver a war message. The Congress declared War against Japan on the same day and on Germany and Italy on 11 December 1941.

By May of 1945, World War Two had been going on for over three years and five months before the Germans surrendered, on 6 May 1945. The Atomic bomb was dropped on Hiroshima on 6 August 1945 and another atomic bombed dropped on Nagasaki on 9 August 1945. On 14 August Japan surrendered. On 2 September 1945 formal ceremonies on board the battleship USS Missouri in Tokyo Bay took place.

The USS Colorado was based in Pearl Harbor from 27 January 1941, and operated in the Hawaiian training area, practicing in intensive exercises and war games until 25 June, when she departed for the west coast and overhaul at Puget Sound Navy Yard, which lasted until 31 March 1942. On 31 May, USS Colorado and USS Maryland set sail from the Golden Gate to form a line of defense against any Japanese attack mounted on San Francisco; the USS Colorado returned to Pearl Harbor on 14 August to complete her preparations for action. She operated in the vicinity of the Fiji Islands and New Hebrides from 8 November 1942 to 17 September 1943 to prevent further Japanese expansion.

During October 1943 she sorted from Pearl Harbor to provide pre-invasion bombardment and fire support for the invasion of Tarawa, returning to port 7 December. After being overhauled, she again provided bombardment and fire support for the Marshall Islands operation that included invasions of Kwajalein and Eniwetok until 23 February 1944.

Joining with other units bound for the Mariana Islands operation at San Francisco, USS Colorado sailed on 5 May 1944 by way of Pearl Harbor and Kwajalein for pre-invasion bombardment and fire support duties at Saipan, Guam, and Tinian from 14 June.

On 24 July 1944, during the shelling of Tinian, Colorado received 22 shell hits from shore batteries, but continued to support the invading troops until 3 August 1944.

After repairs on the west coast, Colorado arrived in Leyte Gulf on 20 November 1944 to support American troops fighting ashore. A week later she was hit by two kamikazes that hit and killed 19 of her men, wounded 72, and caused moderate damage. Never the less as planned, she bombarded Mindoro from 12-17 December 1944 before proceeding to Manus Island for emergency repairs.

USS Colorado returning to Luzon on 1 January 1945 participated in the pre-invasion bombardment in Lingayen Gulf. On 9 January, accidental gunfire hit her superstructure killing 18 and wounding 51. After replenishing at Ulithi, the USS Colorado joined the pre-invasion bombardment group at Kerama Retto on 25 March for the invasion of Okinawa. She remained there supplying fire support until 22 May, when she cleared for Leyte Gulf.

Returning to occupied Okinawa on 6 August 1945, USS Colorado sailed from there for the occupation of Japan, covering the airborne landings. Departing Tokyo Bay on 20 September, she arrived at San Francisco on 15 October, and then steamed to Seattle, Washington, for the Navy-Day celebration on 27 October 1945.

Assigned to Operation Magic Carpet duty, she made three runs to Pearl Harbor to transport 6,357 veterans home before reporting to Bremerton Navy Yard for inactivation. She was placed out of commission in reserve there on 7 January 1947, and sold for scrapping on 23 July 1959. Her bell is currently on display in the University Memorial Center (UMC) at the University of Colorado. (information supplied by Wikipedia, the free encyclopedia).

The following United States Navy Veteran was aboard the USS Colorado during the search for Amelia.

Amelia Earhart 1897-1937, story referenced in back of book

Bottorff, William	United States Navy
Chief Boatswain Mate	World War Two
06/06/1936-1945	Aleutian Islands,
	Dutch Harbor, Alaska

United States Navy Veteran William Bottorff was born on 8 May 1916 in Columbus, Kansas; William turned ninety-seven-years-old in 2013. William was one of six siblings, Mabel 1898-1918; Lois Francis 1899-2008; Charles Franklin 1902-1967; Howard 1906-1918 and Williams' twin Betty Jean 1916-1993, all of Williams siblings are deceased now.

William graduated in 1931 after attending school at King Jack Jr. High School, Kansas and then attended High School at Cherokee County Community High. He remembers much of the Great Depression, Williams

father died during that Depression. When William was sixteen years of age he went out on his own.

Veteran William entered into the United States Navy on 6 June 1936, he was twenty years old, after passing his exams and physical, he was sworn in and shipped to Great Lakes, Illinois for his Basic Training.

After his training was complete, William was transferred to the USS Colorado, while serving on the Colorado he learned how to use a 5" 25 calib 6 ammo anti aircraft gun, then went to Special School aboard the USS Utah and qualified on the 30 calib machine gun, 45 calib machine gun and the 50 calib machine gun.

In 1940 William was out of the service, then rejoined and was station at the United States Submarine Base in the Aleutian Islands, Dutch Harbor, Alaska. While serving at Dutch Harbor, Alaska, William was assigned to base personnel. He was Chief Master at arms, he was Asst. 1st Lt. of base, was as a Chief Boatswain Mate.

The Dutch Harbor base was decommissioned in 1945 and William went on to do training of personnel at Bainbridge, Maryland. Veteran William said that while serving at Dutch Harbor, Alaska, the U.S. Navy Seabees brought in a portable Dry Dock.

William was discharged in the fall of 1945, in Bainbridge, Maryland. For his military service he received the Pacific Theater Medal, the Atlantic Medal along with several other medals and ribbons.

When he returned to civilian life, Navy Veteran William took a position with the Los Angeles Police Department. After being injured while a Police Officer, he went to work for Bank of America.

William's first wife was Florence Evelyn, and they had one child, Linda Ruth Bottorff, and his second wife was Bernice Emmons whom he married in 1961. He is a member of the Masonic Lodge, the Shiners', the Elks and the Sojourners.

William said that the high point of his life was while stationed aboard the U.S.S. Colorado, he was with a group of military personnel to help search for Amelia Earhart for forty-five days.

Veteran William Bottorff, is now retired and living in Irvin, California. I was able to reach him and obtain his military history with assistance of his daughter Honeybee, Linda Joiner who lives in Lakeland, Florida and is a supportive member of Island X-2, Navy Seabees of America.

Albritton, George Edwin

U. S. Army Air Force
World War Two
Navigator on B-29 Superfortress Tinian Island—Japan
05/1942-12/1945

George E. Albritton was born on 31 May 1921, in Polk County, Florida, his parents moved to the West Lake Wales, Florida area when Edwin was four months old. He remains a resident of Lake Wales today with no complaints, except perhaps the 95 degree summer heat. Although Lakes Wales has grown in population, he feels it has not drifted far from pleasurable small town living. He did say native Floridians are becoming a minority.

His own native roots were established with his great grandparents coming from Georgia, to settle south of Mulberry, Florida in 1866. In those early years the family lived off the land, raising cattle in the Fort Drum area and planting seedling citrus groves (most groves now are planted from grafted root stock).

George's father was born in 1883, remembering stories his father told, he relates how 20 to 30 families would gather, usually in December, to haul citrus by ox cart to Tampa. It was a three day round trip, one day to make the trip and sell the crop, the next to buy provisions, the third to trek home. Once in Tampa, the fruit was loaded on a steamer and shipped to New York.

The family's two-story home, built in 1923, is located on the corner of Old Bartow Road and West Lake Wales Road. It remained in the family until its sale in 1988.

George's brother James, still lives near the old homestead and his two sisters, Irma and Mollie reside in Lake Wales. He also has another brother named Franklin D. While growing up there on a citrus grove; Albritton remembers when the Seaboard Railroad Line built the West Lake Wales Depot. A number of the workmen boarded at his parent's home during the construction.

Teen memories include lunching at the soda fountain in Murray's Drug Store and buying a candy bar for a nickel. After high school graduation in 1938, Albritton attended business school in Atlanta, majoring in accounting.

At the time that the Japanese bombed Pearl Harbor he was working in a local real estate insurance office. Edwin enlisted in the Army Air Corps as an aviation cadet in 1942 and was classified as a navigator cadet in May 1942, at Maxwell, and another 12 weeks of advance training at Selman Field, in Monroe, Louisiana, graduating in December 1942; upon graduation he was commissioned a second lieutenant.

He was assigned to the 1st Bomb Squadron, 9th Bomb Group at the Army Air Corps Tactical Air Center, Orlando, Florida, and served as a navigator in B-17 bombers at Brooksville, Florida for 18 months. He was then transferred to McCook, Nebraska in 1944, still in the 1st Bomb Squadron, 9th Bomb Group. Edwin was a staff navigator responsible for the training of sixteen crew navigators in the B-29 Superfortress. The group was deployed to Tinian Island in the Marianas, in the Western Pacific in January 1945; it was the 20th Air Force's strategic bombing campaign against Japan.

Airfields were constructed on the islands of Tinian, Saipan and Guam after the Marianas Islands were wrested from Japanese control in 1944. These airfields became the main bases supporting the large B-29 raids against Japan in the final year of the war. The islands could be easily resupplied by ship.

During the last seven months of World War Two, Edwin participated in the strategic air offensive against Japan, which was a major factor in the Japanese surrender in 1945. He had flown ten combat missions to Japan until August 1945, when hostilities ceased. Edwin was on Tinian during the time that the first atomic bomb quietly arrived on the island, and was loaded into a B-29 flown by another group. Another atomic bomb carried by a B-29 from Tinian convinced the Japanese of the futility of continued resistance, and the war ended in early August 1945. He remained on Tinian until November 1945; then he returned home as a Captain and was assigned to inactive service.

After his military service ended, Edwin became the co-owner and operator of a General Electric appliance store in the building now occupied by Myer's Jewelers, in Lake Wales, Florida. In 1964 he began work for the Lakes Wales Citrus Growers Association, retiring from his position as general manager in 1986.

In 1946, a visit to a doctor's office in Lake Wales provided a cure to both an ailment and bachelorhood. The doctor's receptionist, Barbara Stanland of Waverly, Florida, caught the former navigator's fancy, and they married in 1949. The couple built their permanent residence on the east side of Lakes Wales in 1951. They had one son Robert who is now a Baptist minister in  Raleigh, NC, and a daughter, Julie Dale, who lives in Lakes Wales. The couple has been blessed with four grandchildren, and it could be more since I interviewed him.

Edwin has demonstrated great pride in his heritage and community. He remains a member of the Lake Wales VFW Post 2420, which he joined soon after leaving the Army Air Force. He is a charter member of the Lake Wales Lions Club, joining when the local chapter was established on 24 May, 1949. During his membership he has served the club as its president and in various board positions, he also chaired several key committees. He and Barbara are also active members of the First Presbyterian Church in Lake Wales. George Edwin Albritton has taken much pride in his life serving his country and his community.

SEABEES—(CONSTRUCTION BATTALIONS) of the U.S. NAVY

To most people, Bora Bora, is a Tahitian resort island in the Society Islands chain in the South Pacific. Historically, the island was of great significance to the Allied effort to crush the Japanese during World War Two.

This tropical paradise was a major supply and support base for the U.S. military operations in the South Pacific. The buildings, docks, fueling facilities, roads and airstrips integral to the large military base on this island were among the first accomplishment of the U.S. Navy's famed Construction Battalions, nicknamed the Seabees.

Now the remnants of the Seabee's work have blended into the indigenous features of the island, as the islanders' wartime English helped them transform their island into an international tourist destination.

Bora Bora was the birthplace of the Seabees, military construction forces that would land with the Marines to begin base and infrastructure construction literally upon seizure of land from the enemy. The name of the military operations in the Pacific required bases, fuel depots and airstrips to support coordinated air, ground and naval actions thousands of nautical miles apart.

Before the Seabee's were formed, base construction was the province of civilian construction firms that would use contracted or in-house personnel for the requisite design and construction tasks. However, that was to change with the declaration of war on 8 December 1941. While civilian workers could not be sent into harm's way, the military would need many supply bases throughout the world very quickly.

Admiral Ben Moreell saw this problem coming several weeks before the Japanese bombed Pearl Harbor. His idea was to recruit men with construction skills, put them in uniform, and teach them combat skills. The military liked his idea and soon after Pearl Harbor, he was authorized to start recruiting for the Navy Construction Battalions.

Around the world, the Navy's Seabees established an enviable record for speed and quality of construction under some of the most miserable conditions imaginable. The fact that much of this wartime infrastructure is still used today silently memorializes their skill and sacrifice.

Their "Can Do" spirit was memorialized in the Seabee credo, "The difficult, we do immediately. The impossible, takes a little longer."

The next two veterans in this book served with the U.S. Navy Seabee's during World War Two, also while traveling through this book are several other Veterans that were Navy "Seabee's" during their military service.

Reed, Raymond A. U.S. Navy (Seabee)
28th, 30th, 53rd, 128th, NCB World War Two
& CBD 1040 Iceland, Scotland, Algeria,
09/14/1942-12/26/1945 Tunisia, Southern France,
Hawaii, Guam, Okinawa &
Korea

Ray Reed was born on 22 June, 1923 in Scranton, PA; he grew up in Phillipsburg, New Jersey and attended the Phillipsburg High School along with his two brothers, Robert and John.

The day after Pearl Harbor, Ray went down to the recruiting station to enlist, he was eighteen years old; he was turned down because he only weighed 112 pounds. Ray was told to go home and eat a dozen bananas and to come back when he weighed at least 115. He did, but he didn't put on enough weight until June of 1942.

On 14 September 1942, during the height of World War Two and when the Construction Battalions of the Navy where forming, Ray signed up for the military again this time being accepted. He joined the United States Navy Seabees.

At the time Ray volunteered for military service it was a high point in many areas of the war. On 2 September 1942, Rommel was driven back by Montgomery in the Battle of Alam Halfa and around 13 September 1942 the Battle of Stalingrad had begun.

After his physical he was sworn in and told to report for Basic Training at Camp Bradford, Norfolk, VA, although he was technically assigned to CBD1040; as a Second Class Boatswain's Mate; he also had served with several Constructions Battalions, (the Seabees).

During his military career Ray traveled to several military bases; Iceland, Scotland, Algeria, Tunisia, Hawaii, Guam, Okinawa and Korea, his most noted experience during the War was that of D-Day, the Normandy Invasion.

There were actually two invasions then, Normandy and Southern France that started 6 June 1944. Ray went in on the second invasion in Southern France, on 15 August 1944.

The story is that on the 6th day of June 1944 all the troops loaded up in North Africa, but it was two-pronged, "a little-known fact" Ray said. What happened is that they didn't have enough LSTs (landing ship tanks) that carry tanks and also soldiers.

Nine times out of 10 they would hit a sandbar, and they still had 100 yards of water from there to the beach. It was their job, the Navy Seabees—to line causeways up so the troops could go over the causeways right onto the beach.

On 7 May 1945 an unconditional surrender of all German forces to Allies and on 8 May, V-E (Victory in Europe) Day occurred.

Although the war had ended in Europe, the war in the Pacific was still going on until 6 August 1945 when the first Atomic bomb was dropped on Hiroshima, Japan, and on 9 August 1945 the second Atomic bomb dropped on Nagasaki, Japan; followed by the unconditional surrender by the Japanese on 14 August 1945. The surrender agreement was signed on 2 September 1945.

On 26 December 1945 after the war ended, Ray Reed was discharged from the US Navy, during his military career he had earned the French Legion of Honor, Good Conduct Medal, Combat Ribbon, American Theater Ribbon, European Theater Ribbon w/2 battle stars, Pacific Theater Ribbon w/2 battle stars, Victory Ribbon, Korean Occupation Medal, and Expert Rifle Medal.

After the military, Ray married Ethel and pursued the occupation of that of a Printer. He likes to play golf and is an active member of the Seabee Veterans of America.

On January 2009, Ray was awarded France's top honor from the French Ambassador to the United States stating that he had been chosen for Frances highest honor—the Legion d'Honneur or French Legion of Honor award.

Ray Reed and 28 former servicemen were honored in a formal ceremony held in Naples, Florida in late March 2009, at the Edison College Campus, several hundred friends and family members attended the ceremony. He was in France then, and appreciated what they did, but never expected this after 65 years, he said.

The letter that was presented by Ambassador de France read:

Dear Mr. Reed, I am pleased to inform you that by a decree signed by the President of the French Republic on 19 December 2008, you have been named a "Chevalier" of the Legion of Honor.

The award testifies to the President of the French Republic's high esteem for your merits and accomplishments. In particular, it is a sign of France's true and unforgettable gratitude and appreciation for your personal, precious contribution to the United States decisive role in the liberation of our country during World War II.

The Legion of Honor was created by Napoleon in 1802 to acknowledge services rendered to France by persons of great merit. The French people will never forget your courage and your devotion to the great cause of freedom.

It is a personal pleasure for me to convey to you my sincere and warm congratulations.

Sincerely, Pierre Vimont

While interviewing Ray, I asked him what the high point of his life was. He told me that being selected to receive the French Legion of Honor Award on 28 March 2009.

Ray Reed and his wife Ethel are residents of North Ft. Myers, Florida.

Muller, Edward P.	U. S. Navy (Seabee)
98th NCB, First Class Cook	World War Two
11/ 1942-03/23/46	Tarawa, Hawaii, Japan

Edward was born on 12 February (President Lincoln's B-Day), in Garfield, New Jersey, after High School he attended several culinary schools in New Jersey and New York. Ed grew up during the depression and he can recall that going to the local movie only cost five cents and you could buy cigarettes for a nickel.

In November of 1942 Ed was nineteen years old; he signed up for the United States Navy Seabees and accomplished his basic training in Davisville, Rhode Island. After basic training Ed Muller was transferred to Eva Beach Barracks in Honolulu, then to the Island of Maui in Hawaii to train with the 2nd Marine Corps Division. The military then took 400 of the Seabees, fully armed, supplied them with Marine uniforms and shipped them out to invade Tarawa.

Tarawa is in the Gilbert Islands.

On the morning of 20 November 1943 the first wave of Marines went in on the amphibious tractors that Marines called LVT's or Amtrak's, and they made it, but after that the low tide caused the flat bottomed Higgins boats to hang up onto the reefs, which were covered with only three feet of water. This made the Marines and Seabee's easy targets for the enemy's firepower. The troops had to wade 500 yards to the shoreline, and only half made it. The ones that made it ashore had to deal with the 4,500 Japanese concealed in sand covered concrete bunkers.

Next to Ed's galley was a 12'X12'X7' deep foxhole. This made it very convenient for them to dive in during the bombing. During the battle Ed received seven bombing cuts on his right side; fortunately they healed without too much trouble.

Even before the fighting ceased they were working to put the enemy air strips into shape. The US troops secured Tarawa at the cost of nearly 1,000 killed and another 2,300 wounded. After Tarawa the Americans learned the value of advance bombardment.

The Island was secured by 23 November, and four days after the initial strike on Tarawa their planes were using the air field that the Navy Seabees rebuilt. Unfortunately the losses were high but the commanders were aware of the enemy's strength.

In a Directive dated 24 December 1943, NCB 98 was commended by Adm. Hoover. Congratulations were expressed to all the Seabees for making new landing fields available for large planes in "such good time". Also Secretary of the Navy, F. Knox thanked all who participated in landing on Tarawa.

Early in 1945 his Battalion, the 98th Navy Construction Battalion was shipped back to Maui to train for another invasion.

On 9 August 1945 the atomic bomb was dropped on Nagasaki, Japan, five days later Ed's Battalion were boarded again and shipped out to Japan to help clean up the terrible mess that the bomb left.

On 2 September 1945 Japan surrendered. Navy Seabee Edward Muller was honorably discharged and returned to the states and his hometown the day after Christmas, 1945.

Ed attended culinary institutions in every state where he was stationed throughout his military career, and he also attended some in New Jersey during the 1960's.

For his military service during World War Two, Edward Muller received the Asiatic Pacific Medal w/1 Star, the Good Conduct Medal, the American Theater Medal, the Victory Medal and the Combat Action Ribbon among others.

After his military career, Ed returned to his former position as welder in Okonite, Paterson, NJ until 1964. Then he schooled as a professional driver using auto carriers to deliver cars for M&G Convoy (Chrysler Corp.) until retiring in 1985.

He was the Commander of Catholic War Veterans, Clifton, NJ, during the late 50's and officer of the Boy Scouts of America the same period.

Ed was an officer in Sussex, NJ, and BPOE from the early 1980's until 1999. The Muller's wintered in Florida from 1985 to 1999 and Ed managed the kitchen in the community where they lived and also worked as a chef at Bonita Springs, Florida Elks.

He has been member of Island X-8, Ft. Myers since 1997 and has been 1st. Vice Commander since 2002. Since 2000 Ed has been very active in his community (Island Club) in the kitchen, Treasurer of the Bingo Committee, and served on the Election, Safety, Architectural and Volunteers Committee.

Ed and his wife June; of 66 years reside in Estero, Florida; they had three sons, Donald a US Navy Veteran, Kenneth the second born, is disabled from injuries he received while serving in Vietnam and their youngest son Richard who passed away at fifty-seven years of age.

Edward P. Muller said that he has no regrets, and the high points of his life include RV travel through entire US and Canada, as well as extensive world traveling, missing only India, Egypt, Africa and a very few other smaller countries.

FLYING FORTRESS—BOEING B-17—The Boeing B-17 Flying Fortress is a four-engine heavy bomber aircraft developed in the 1930's for the U. S. Army Air Corps (USAAC).

The B-17 was primarily employed by the U.S. Army Air Forces in the daylight precision strategic bombing campaign of World War II against German industrial and military targets.

The B-17 also participated to a lesser extent in the War in the Pacific, early in World War II, where it conducted raids against Japanese shipping and airfields.

National origin, United States, manufacturer Boeing, first flight 28 July 1935, Retired 1968, Number built 12,731, produced 1936-1945. Wikipedia. org

Lamb, James "Troy"-B-17 Pilot U.S. Army Air Corp
81ˢᵗ Bomber Group.-   World War Two
534ᵗʰ Bomber Sq
02/17/1943-11/06/1945   England, London, Scotland
                            Czechoslovakia

Troy, as everyone knows him, remembers the depression while growing up in Frostproof, Florida along with his three sisters and one brother. He mentioned that his father was the only one that remained on the payroll during the summer months with the fruit industry. He also remembers his parents were very humble, he never heard a curse word out of them.

Troy came to life in the spring on 11 April 1923; he is now ninety years old. He was born in Georgia and raised and attended schools in Frostproof, Florida. Troy's two favorite teachers were Ms. Cooper and Ms. Webb. He enjoyed playing sports, especially baseball. He also recalled making and playing with homemade guns, they made them with rubber and used their imagination.

In February 1943 the wars in the Pacific and Europe were going full course at the time when Troy was drafted at age nineteen years. His friend Gussie Sullivan was also drafted and so they went in together.

They were examined in Atlanta, Georgia then transferred to an Army Base in Anderson, Alabama. Next they were transported to Birmingham, Alabama for further testing. Upon acceptance Troy was transferred to

Miami Beach and then to Spearfish, South Dakota, where he learned preflight training.

In Marfa, Texas, Troy began Advance Flight Training with twin engines, and flew solo. His advance training took place in Yuma, Arizona, Visual, California and the last training took place in Tampa, Florida at Haven Park, he was assigned to the 534 Bomber Sq. Group.

On 24 March 1945 Troy was transported to England on the Queen Elizabeth for his first over-seas assignment, from the ship he was taken by train to Scotland. Troy said that while traveling through England he witnessed children begging for food. During WW II, England had been so heavily bombed by the Germans, and most of the people that lived there became homeless; Troy said, he was able to give the children some candy.

Arriving in Scotland, Troy, boarded another train which took him to an Air Force Base near London; this final destination is where he practiced bombing missions in preparation for over-seas bombing on Japan. Fortunately, the bombing mission that he would have been part of was canceled due to the atomic bomb.

While Troy was waiting for his next assignment he visited the local movies in Whittington, England, and to his surprise came upon another fellow that he went to school with in Frostproof.

Before Troy was transferred back to America he had flown a mission over Czechoslovakia and was shot at. He was also assigned to a group that had the mission of air-lifting POW's to France.

In May 1945, Troy returned to the United States, arriving in Maine, he was given a furlough, and then traveled to South Dakota, where he received his military discharge on 6 November 1945. For his military service he received several medals and ribbons.

When Troy returned home to Frostproof after the war ended he started his own wholesale business. He sold candy and tobacco in 1946, later the business flourished into a wholesale food business that he operated for over forty years; until 1988 when he sold it.

I questioned Troy as to why he didn't continue his flying career when he returned home after the war, he explained that was his interest until he learned that in order to rent an airplane it cost $9.00 an hour, which was a great deal of money back then. However, he did have much success with his alternative, the food business.

In 1946, Troy married Grace; a marriage that lasted fifty-six years, until Grace succumbed to cancer in 2002. They had three children, Marylyn, James Jr. and Edward. They had seven grandchildren and several great-grandchildren.

After Troy retired he started working part-time at his son's (James Jr.) insurance agency; his other son Edward is a minister in Littleton, NC. Troy and his new bride Brenda live in Lake Wales, Florida where they enjoy doing senior activities.

Edward L. Allen
2nd Class Petty Officer
03/1943-03/1946

1950-1952 (called back)

United States Navy
World War Two (Seabee)
So. Pacific, Guadalcanal,
Solomon Islands, also,
New Caledonia, Tulagi,
Emirau
Korean War
U.S.N, 6th Fleet, USS
DesMoines (heavy cruiser)

Ed Allen was born at the foot of the mountains in Spartanburg, South Carolina on 5 March 1925, it is also where he went to school and grew up until his parents moved to Miami, Florida, and then they moved to Atlanta, Georgia. He has two sisters, his older sister passed away and his younger sister lives in Atlanta, Georgia; her name is Jean. Jean was an Air Line Stewardess for Delta Airlines before her retirement.

Ed's family was living in Orlando, Florida when Ed turned eighteen years old, back then it was a law that when you turned eighteen years old, that you had to sign up for the draft, and it wasn't long before he was called to duty, he told me that he hadn't had a chance to finish school before being drafted, but did finish his schooling after he came home from the war.

The Seabee insignia is a bee blazing away with a Tommy gun while carrying a wrench and hammer, their principal weapon was the "bulldozer", one of which was known as "Old Faithful", during World War Two it saw so much action throughout the Pacific that the Seabees hoped eventually, to parade it down the streets of Tokyo.

In the summer of 1943, after being inducted into the U.S. Navy Seabees, and being sworn in, Ed was transported to Camp Allen, Norfolk, Virginia to do his basic training. Ed had to admit that at training they were novices, that the constant and intense drilling was an ordeal with tired muscle and burning feet, but they were willing to train, so that they could serve our country.

They resented that the enemy had forced them to leave their homes, family and brought them to mingle with strangers, to shoulder rifles and heavy packs, and to march, march and more marching; up and down the field, hour after hour.

They practiced maneuvers on Virginia Shores, they learned to use rifles, and had combat training. Ed Allen also trained in Davisville, RI and Gulfport, Mississippi. He learned about engines, generators, refrigerators, they learned how to build roads, bridges, quonset huts, temporary hospitals, and much more.

After finishing much of his necessary training Ed was placed with the 116th NCB, but it wasn't long before he was switched to the 27th NCB, because the 27th Navy Construction Battalion had lost most of their Seabees due to deaths, injuries, and most of all, disease's, such as malaria, jungle rot, and other war-time physical ailments.

Ed's first duty station was Guadalcanal, soon after arriving on the Island they had the backbreaking job of unloading what was bought in by LCTs in drums (gas). The drums were very heavy; they worked all day in the boiling sun, day after day. Then they began the construction of a camp.

Guadalcanal-Construction Work

Construction work was centered around Henderson Field and the Naval Operating Base at Lunga and Koli Point on Guadalcanal.

The extension and improvement of Henderson field absorbed the majority of the effort, especially for the first elements of the Construction Battalions.

The island hopping war the allies fought in the South Pacific depended in large measure on a rough-and-ready breed of engineers who proudly called themselves "the toughest road gang in history". The Seabees being versatile performers could magically transform the thickest jungle or most barren atoll into an air and naval base within a matter of days, plus build roads and clear underwater obstacles, with the speed that became legendary throughout the Pacific; usually while under enemy fire. After the war they continued to use their trades and skills in civilian life.

From Guadalcanal Ed's Battalion went to Tulagi Harbor, Solomon Islands; the island was primarily of volcanic ash formation, rising sharply from the water, to the elevation of 250 feet. Half the Island consisted of mangrove swamps, twisted trees with tangles and big roots. The other half of the island had natural coral overlying the island reef, and everywhere was red clay. They blasted ash from the hills to fill in the swamp, and Ed said in the process the acid rising was a problem; it actually made the men sick.

The Seabees also did work on nearby Florida Island, there they did the impossible. They built a road going upward from the beach at a steep angle to the top of a 600 foot hill. The road was to be two miles long, up and down, mostly up, and the stuff they were making it with was red gumbo-like clay that held water like a sponge.

The frequent rain made the roadbed stinking and steaming, they had to pave it with teakwood and mahogany logs, to make the road at all passable, and most of the timbers were 80 to 90 feet long. The road was being built for the Marines.

Engineers had told them the task was impossible, but they did it. Yes, the "CAN DO" spirit was memorialized in the Seabee credo, "The difficult, we do immediately. The impossible takes a little longer." And before leaving Florida's Island they built a permanent camp for the Marines, at Lyons Point. It was adequate for a thousand men.

After Tulagi, they were told that they were going in on an invasion on Emirau Island, (they were told that 60,000 Japanese were on the Island), fortunately when they arrived, they were surprised to learn that the enemy had moved on.

Once again the 27th CB began setting up camp on the Island. One major task that the Seabees learned to do was repairing of ships that had been damaged. They were not ship fitters when they left America. A great many of the Seabees had never seen an oceangoing vessel until they boarded the one that took them overseas.

After the inferno of Guadalcanal a small flotilla of LCTs (landing craft for tanks) came across Sealark Channel for nearly a year; the ships came to the 27th CB stationed at the Island. And it was the Seabees that learned to heal the ships; they came to the 27th for repairs and a chance to fight again.

The 27th CB with the help of the 63rd CB built a theatre on Emirau, big enough to hold two battalions; they were able to watch movies, and later they had to enlarge it to be able to accommodate more battalions. When they learned that Bob Hope was coming, the crew built a stage and dressing rooms, foot lights and back drops. One Monday night in August Bob Hope arrived, 7,000 gathered to see the entertainer with accomplices Patty Thomas, Jerry Colonna and Frances Langford.

The Navy Seabees were seldom given R & R, and when they did get it, they would go to New Zealand, for rest and entertainment. Ed Allen expressed that he enjoyed traveling around New Zealand taking in the sights.

After two years of work and war they came home, returning from Guadalcanal, Tulagi, and Emirau and other smaller South Pacific Islands, to rest from fighting and toil, to see their families again. They were proud of the work they accomplished, the roads they built through mud and swamp and jungle, the earth and rock and coral they excavated.

They are proud of what they achieved, the bridges and docks and hospitals plus other constructed facilities. They did this while being shot at, bombed and other hazards. They had helped in paving the road to Tokyo and ending World War Two.

After Ed's discharge in March of 1946, it was mandatory for the troops being discharged to still remain on Inactive Service for six years. Ed did return to school to earn his diploma, then he went on to Florida Votec, he also attended Tri State College in Indiana after the war where he studied mechanics.

In 1950 when trouble was brewing in Korea, Ed was called back to serve once again with the U.S. Navy Seabees. For the two years that he served during the Korean War, Ed was stationed on the U.S.S. DesMoines, a Heavy Cruiser with the 6th Fleet, where he worked as a mechanic on the ship. He also had the opportunity to meet General D.D. Eisenhower; later United States President Eisenhower, when he visited the 6th Fleet, while on the ship.

When Ed was finally released from the military for the second time, he obtained employment with the JTB Company, later changed to John Bean Company. The company made heavy equipment for the Citrus Industry. Ed stayed with the company for thirty-two years, before retiring.

Ed Allen now lives in Lakeland, Florida, he never was married, but manages to take care of himself, and he said he learned how to cook while serving in the military on the Islands. He once owned the property where the Lakeland Museum is now located.

Although I say he lives alone, he is not really alone, Ed is very fond of "cats" and he has many of them that live with him. You can usually find him sitting out on his porch enjoying his senior years and watching the "cats" playing. Thank you, Edward L. Allen for your military service and our American Freedom.

History of the Mighty Eighth Air Force

The Eighth Bomber Command (Re-designated 8th AF in February 1944) was activated as part of the United States Army Air Forces 28 January 1942, at Hunter Field in Savannah. In February, the next month the Eighth AF was taken to England to prepare for its mission of conducting aerial bombardment missions against Nazi-occupied Europe.

During World War II, under the leadership of such Generals as Eaker and Jimmy Doolittle, the 8th AF became the greatest air armada in history.

At its peak, the 8th AF could dispatch more than 2,000 four-engine bombers and 1,000 fighters on a single mission. For these reasons, the 8th AF became known as the "Mighty Eighth". (reference from museum of the Mighty Eighth Air Force).

Operation Tidal Wave was an air attack by bombers of the U.S. Army Air Forces (USAAF) based in Libya on nine oil refineries around Ploiesti, Romania on 1 August 1943, during WWII. It was a strategic bombing mission and part of the "oil campaign" to deny petroleum-based fuel to the Axis. The mission resulted in "no curtailment of overall product output", and so was deemed unsuccessful.

This mission was one of the costliest for the USAAF in the European Theater, and 53 aircraft and 660 air crewmen lost. It was the worst loss ever suffered by the USAAF on a single mission, and its date was later referred to as "Black Sunday".

The second Schweinfurt raid-was a World War II air battle that took place over Germany between forces of the United States 8th Air Force and German Luftwaffe's fighter arm. The aim of the American-led mission was a strategic bombing raid on ball bearing factories in order to reduce production of these vital parts for all manner of war machines.

Planners added additional fighter escorts to cover the outward and return legs of the operations, and sent the entire force against Schweinfurt alone, instead of splitting the force. Despite these tactical modifications, a series of minor mishaps combined with the ever-increasing efficiency of the German anti-aircraft efforts proved to be devastating.

American History of the Army Air Forces in the Second World War acknowledged losses had been so heavy the USAAF would not return to the target for four months.

The Mighty Eighth compiled an impressive record in the war. This achievement, however, carried a high price. The 8th AF suffered one-half of the U.S. Army Air Forces' causalities in World War II (47,000-plus casualties with more than 26,000 deaths).

There were 261 fighter Aces and 305 gunner Aces in the Eighth in World War II. Thirty-one of those fighter aces exceeded 15 or more aircraft kills.

After the war in Europe in July 1945, the 8th AF headquarters moved to Okinawa, where it trained new bomber groups for combat against Japan. The Japanese, however, surrendered before the 8th AF saw action in the Pacific Theater.

In June 1946, the headquarters moved to McDill Field, Florida, to become part of the newly established Strategic Air Command. In November 1950, the 8th AF headquarters transferred to Forth Worth Army Field (later Carswell Air Force Base) in Texas. (National Museum of the Mighty Eighth Air Force)

The following U. S. Veteran served with the 8th Air Force, during WW II.

Santoro, Cpl. Sal N.	United States Air Force
8th Air Force, B-24 Liberator	World War Two
2nd Bombardment Div.	N.France, Normandy,
Air Offensive Europe Ltr ETO	Germany, Ardennes
03/10/1943-10/18/1945	Central Europe

Sal was born in Massachusetts on 3 March 1923; the son of John and Katy Santoro, they also had eleven other children that grew up and attended schools in Somerville, Massachusetts. Sal lost his mother at an early age in his and her life; he lived with his father until his father asked Sal to leave school at age 16 years to join the Civilian Conservation Corps (C.C.C), a Government Program that President F.D. Roosevelt implemented in 1932-1942 to put people to work.

Civilian Conservation Corps-referenced in back of book!

Sal signed up for the U.S. Air Force on 10 March 1943, during World War Two. Also serving in the military during World War Two was two of his brothers, John Santoro, of the Medics in Germany and Cpl. Steve Santoro, with the infantry in Italy. After Sal was militarily processed and passed his entire Basic Training tests, he was assigned to the Eighth Air Force.

From December 1943 until 12 May 1945 Sal served overseas, and was an assistant crew chief in a B-24 Liberator Squadron ordnance department, which played a vital role in the Eighth Air Force's tremendous task of delivering tons of bombs on Germany.

Although classified as an aviation munitions worker, he is popularly known as a "bomb jockey". He and the men of his section are skilled in the scientific handling of high-explosive and incendiary bombs, and these ordinance technicians are on duty long with irregular hours, the majority of which are at night under the strictest black-out conditions. The bombs, ranging from 100-pound general purpose "babies" to 2000-pound "block busters," are  handled by hand with the aid of special winches for accurate placement in the bomb-bay racks. After the scheduled fusing, a specialist of delicate fuses then inserts them into the cavities at the nose and tail of the bomb.

Finally the entire load is carefully checked by Cpl. Santoro to ascertain if it is ready for the strenuous flight to enemy territory. The squadron of which he is a member was recently cited by Maj. Gen. William E. Kepner, Commanding General of the Second Bombardment Division, for "outstanding performance of duty" in flying 82 consecutive combat missions without loss of aircraft or personnel, thereby bettering the former safe-flying record of 68 missions held since last spring by a squadron from another group.

His ordnance organization is attached to the 453rd Bomb Group, which received a division citation upon completion of its first 100 combat missions. During a period of five months, bombers of the group dropped more than 4000 tons of bombs and destroyed more than 50 enemy aircraft in the air.

During his tour of duty Sal was in Air Offensive Europe B-24 Liberator Group (Ltr), European Theatre of Operation (ETO), February 1944; North France Ltr ETO, January 1945, Normandy Ltr ETO, February 1945, Germany Ltr ETO, April 1945, Ardennes Central Europe TWX AGO Washington DC. His decorations, awards include the Good Conduct Medal, SO 188 Sta 2 AF, August 44 and EAME Theater Service Medal and w/6 Bronze Stars.

Cpl. Sal Santoro separated from the Army Air Force on 18 October 1945 with an Honorable Discharge. He returned to his home town in Somerville, MA. Being a civilian once again, Sal went to Automotive School, while working for a bottling company. He went to California and worked as an Auto Mechanic at Baines Bike Shop 1952, and worked his way up to Assistant Manager, he was also School Assistant and after seven years he went back to Massachusetts. He took a position as material handler that lasted for twenty-three years; in 1988 he worked at Langley Company as a Parts Service Manager.

Sal started "roller-skating" when he was sixteen year old, he skated in eight states in the U.S., and while in the Air Force and stationed in England, when on leave he enjoyed roller skating in London. He retired and moved to Florida in 1997, and continued skating at several skating rinks in Florida.

I met Sal at Reflections Skating Rink, in Kissimmee, Florida. He skated the dance-steps with his beautiful wife Anna. Sal retired from skating when he was eighty-nine years old. Sal and Anna also went dancing at the Senior Center in St. Cloud, Florida. Since he said; he is too old to skate anymore, Sal bowls these days with an average of 130-150 and also exercises at their home in Winter Haven, Florida everyday.

Sal is the father of four children, three girls, Nancy, Cindy, Missy and Sal Jr. Veteran Sal Santoro said he has no regrets and much to be thankful for.

4th **Armored Division (United States)** The division was activated on 15 April 1941 by cadre of the 1st Armored Division, and was fitted out as a full armored division in 1942. The 4th Armored Division deployed to the United Kingdom in early 1944 in preparation for the invasion of France.

After training in England from January to July 1944, the 4th Armored Division landed at Utah Beach 11 July and entered combat 17 July. After helping secure the Coutances area in France on 28 July the division then swung south to take Nantes, cutting off the Brittany Peninsula, 12 August 1944. Turning east, it drove swiftly across France north of the Loire, smashed across the Moselle 11-13 September, flanked Nancy and captured Luneville, 16 September.

It fought several German Panzer grenadier brigades in the Lorraine area including the SS Panzer grenadier Brigade 49 and SS Panzer grenadier Brigade 51 at this time, defeating a larger German force through superior tactics and training.

After more fighting from 27 September to 11 October, the division rested briefly, returning to combat 9 November, attacking through to Dieuze and crossed the Saar River, to establish and expand bridgehead and took

Singling, Bining and Baerendorf in November, they were relieved on 8 December 1944.

Two days after the Germans launched their Ardennes offensive, the 4th Armored entered the fight, racing northwest into Belgium. The 4th attacked the Germans at Bastogne, they continued their pursuit of the enemy crossing several rivers and by 6 May the division crossed into Czechoslovakia, established a bridgehead across the Octave River at Strakonice, with forward elements at Pisek. It was reassigned to the XII Corps on in 1945. The 4th Armored Division lost 1, 519 men while fighting in World War Two.

On 14 June 1945, at Landshut, Germany, the Fourth Armored became the only tank division and the second entire division in the U.S. Army history to be decorated by order of the President, General Devers officially decorated the division's colors just 79 days after the War Department first announced the award would be given to the Fourth Armored. At that time, 28 March; the impatient Fourth Armored was in the midst of one of its typical spearhead drives for General Patton's Army. The troops were assembled for review for all its battle accomplishments.

The 6 X 6 trucks rolled through Landshut all morning on the way to the field at the foot of the bluff overlooking the Isar Valley. The trucks parked in columns' and the troops jumped out grinning and calling to each other. The tankers wiped off their submachine guns and the infantry men blew last specks of dust from their worn garlands. At 1300 the engineers put the finishing touches on the reviewing stand and five-wide-truck mediums from "B" Company, 8th Tank Battalion rumbled into line behind the big Fourth Armored sign that had "France, Belgium, Luxembourg, Germany, Czechoslovakia painted on it. The band was poised to play the old marches "The Star Spangled Banner"—Fourth Armored men who fought through World War Two stood ready for their finest and last review together.

The veterans of Fourth Armored marched well on the conquered German soil that day. In battle-stained combat jackets, mud-spattered tank helmets, rank after rank swept past the reviewing stand, the men who fought through five countries marched for those who were not there. (ref. Wikipedia.org)

Below you will read about a veteran that served with the 4th Armored Division, he was assigned to Company "A", the 37th Tank Battalion.

Parzyck, Vincent   United States Army
POM/MPOV   World War Two
37th Tank Div.4th Armored Div.
10/25/44-08/12/46   Germany

Vincent was born on 18 July 1926, he grew up in Burlington, New Jersey and at the age of eighty-seven years is still a resident there. He and his wife Theresa had two sons, Vincent Paul and Ronald Wayne. Vincent remembers much of the depression while growing up, he said that his family was very poor as most families were.

From age fifteen to eighteen Vincent was an Air Raid Warden in his neighborhood. On 18 July 1944 Vincent turned eighteen, in October of that year he was drafted into the United States Army; he was processed at Fort Dix, New Jersey and shipped to Fort Knox, Kentucky for six weeks of basic training.

After completing his basic training, Vincent was shipped to Ft. Meade, Maryland, then onto Camp Kilmer, New Jersey. In New York he boarded merchant marine ship USS Sea Robin (troop ship) that took the new troops to Le Havre, France. In January 1945, Vincent was assigned to Company "A", 37th Tank Battalion, 4th Armored Division.

In March his 37th Tank Battalion hooked up with General Patton's' Division in Blatna, Czechoslovakia. After the initial hook up with the

Fourth, Vincent served in different locations in Germany, Neumarkt,  Nurnberg, Bamberg, Stuttgart, Vilshofen, Munich, Deggendorf, etc.; during his engagement with the 37th. Tank Battalion, Vincent experienced the most fighting in Blatna, Czechoslovakia.

After the World War Two ended, the 4th Armored was disbanded and formed into the 37th Battalion, 83rd Squadron in Hanau, Germany in January 1946 and served in Weisbaden, Landshut, Regensburg, Germany, etc. in the motor pool, converting all the Army equipment to the constabulary units with the Yellow letter "C" as peace keeping units. Vincent was discharged on 12 August 1946, he returned home aboard Army Troop Ship USS United States. For his service in the United States Army Vincent earned the WW II Victory Medal, one Battle Star and several other medals and ribbons. He also received from France, the French Croix de Guerre (a military decoration for bravery).

Returning to civilian life Vincent took a position with the New Jersey Electric and Gas Company (PSE&G), a position he held for forty-years. I asked Vincent if he had any regrets, he said none; he is a Life Member of the VFW (Veterans of Foreign Wars), Masonic Fraternity, Good Sam Club (life), Family Motor Coach, National Camping Travelers Club, Scottish Rite and the Crescent Shrine for Cripple Children.

Military camps bordering local towns conducted block parties during nice weather, in order to provide diversion and entertainment for the troops before they were shipped off to war. A play named Biloxi Blue's, staged by Private Neil Simon later captured life in such southern camps.

Also, American spirits were cheered-up with big band music such as Jimmy and Tommy Dorsey, the Arthur Murray Dance Studios, Bob Crosby's movie "Road to Morocco", songs, "Don't Sit Under the Apple Tree", "Praise the Lord" and Pass the Ammunition and "Remember Pearl

Harbor", they sang for strength, one of the most favored was a number by Raymond B. Egan, music by Richard Whiting in 1918, titled "Till We Meet Again".

Theodore W. (Ted)Beals
United States Navy
World War Two
Navigations &Visual
Communications'
Korea
06/1945-11/1966 "Submarines"

In Central Pennsylvania, near the top of the Allegheny Mountains lies a small town given the name Moshannon. It is the town that Ted's father came home to after he had served in the military during World War One (he was stationed along the Mexican Border). It is the town where Mr. Beal's owned and operated a small grocery store. It is the town where Theodore (Ted) W. Beal was born, it is the town where Ted grew up and went to school in.

Ted attended grade school in the small town, he stated that during grade school he only had two teachers, the first teacher he had was from the first grade (they didn't have kindergarten) thru the fourth grade, and the second teacher taught him from the fifth grade through the eight grade. He said that before you were promoted to go to High School, you were required to pass an examination.

Ted also had seven siblings, four sisters, and three brothers. Growing up in such a large family during the depression you would think that one would have memories of lacking some of the basic necessities from time to time. However, he had no memories of ever going hungry or lacking adequate clothing. They had a large garden and grew a lot of their food.

He remembered they would fill up the space behind the steps to the cellar with potatoes in the fall and they would last all winter. He told me that they were never forced to eat what they didn't want to; like many of that era. At Christmas time they usually received one toy and the remainder of the gifts was clothing. The only thing he could remember wanting badly and never receiving was a two wheeled bicycle. But he was able to survive without it.

They had no organized sports (until High School), so they made their own entertainment. They played the usual neighborhood games and would swim at the local swimming hole in the summertime; a favorite. During the hunting season his father would go hunting for two weeks, at which time Ted and older sister Dorothy would be responsible for tending to his grocery store. During his father's later years Ted had asked him how he managed to raise such a large family during the depression. His only comment was "I always paid my bills on time".

After grade school Ted attended High School in Kylerstown, Pennsylvania, and in June just before his eighteenth birthday and with his parent's signature Ted volunteered for the military service, at that time World War Two was in progress. He said that all his brothers also signed up for the military, two were active during World War Two, and two served afterwards. His brother Evan could have avoided going into the military service.

He had been an employee at Martin Aircraft, (later Lockheed Martin) as a machinist; the company was a high priority during the war. His brother found out that the company had gotten him a deferment, Evan was upset because they didn't ask him first. He quit the company and joined the military. He was assigned to the 82nd Airborne as a Glider Trooper during and at the Battle of the Bulge.

The 82nd Airborne Infantry Division was reactivated at Camp Claiborne, Louisiana under the command of Major General Omar Bradley. On 15

August 1942 the division took wings as the 82nd Airborne Division. By the time they went overseas, the 82nd consisted of the 325th Glider Infantry Regiment and the 504th and 505th Parachute Infantry.

Battle of the Bulge—The Ardennes Offensive, On 16 December 1944 the Germans launched a surprise offensive through the Ardennes Forest which caught the Allies completely by surprise. The 82nd moved into action on 17 December in response to the German's Ardennes Counter offensive and blunted General Von Runstedt's northern penetration in the American lines. On 20th December the 82nd attacked in the Vielsalm-St Vith region and the 504th PIR took Monceau. This fierce attack forced the German units back across the Ambleve River the next day.

Ted told me that the one regret that he has in life is that he didn't question his brother Evan about his experiences while serving at the Battle of the Bulge.

Now when Ted was called on to take his physical in June 1945, he was asked to line up for the doctor, after looking at Ted's back, the doctor tapped him on the shoulder and said he had flunked the physical. He was told that one of his legs was shorter than the other. Some people would welcome the chance not to have to go and fight, especially today. But not Ted, Ted found out what had to be done and corrected it with a raised shoe. He was now accepted into the US Navy. It wasn't until 1949 that he experienced back spasms from the defect.

Ted Beal accomplished his basic training in Bainbridge, Maryland, and then attended Signalmen School at Great Lakes, IL, also completing submarine school at Groton, CT. When he completed all his training he was assigned and served as a Navigator and Communicator aboard six different submarines for a period of twenty-one years.

Although once he was asked to serve duty outside the submarine service for three years as an instructor with the N.R.O.T.C. (Naval Reserve Officer Training Corps) program, at Yale University.

He served aboard the U.S.S. Segundo (SS 398), U.S.S. Grouper (SSK 214), U.S.S. Cusk (U.S.S. 348), U.S.S. Tambor (SS 198), U.S.S. Batfish (SS 310), U.S.S. Harder (SS 568), Staff, Commander Submarine Force, Atlantic Fleet.

During the Korean War he served on the West Coast with Submarine assignments. The U.S.S. Grouper (SSK-214) was the first submarine modified to be an antisubmarine submarine. As new Sonar was designed it would be installed on the Grouper and then the new sonar would be tested in Bermuda waters during the summer months and Iceland waters in the winter, after WWII in the fifties. The submarines carried a crew of seventy or eighty men.

Ted recalled a near disaster during a run when he was nearly washed overboard. He was the first one up when the submarine surfaced to look out at the side for ships, the ledge that he would grab hold of was very small, he was nearly washed overboard due to a wave coming up. The submarines had diesel engines.

In November of 1966, Ted Beal retired from the US Navy, for his service he was awarded several medals that included the American Campaign, World War Two National Defense Service Medal, World War Two Victory Medal, Naval Occupation Medal, and Good Conduct Medal.

After being retired from the Navy, Ted worked for a defense contractor for four years; building submarines. Then he obtained a position in a Public Accounting Firm. He worked during the daytime and in the evening attended classes to obtain a degree. He attended Mitchell College, New London, CT (received Associate Degree), Quinnipiac College, Hamden, CT (Bachelor Degree), at the age of forty-four.

Ted also was awarded a Certified Public Account Certificate in January 1975, at the age of 47. He retired in 1990 as President of his firm. Ted was also an Adjunct Professor of accounting at the University of Connecticut, at Avery Point in Groton, CT.

Ted said that the high point in his life was being selected to serve on Admirals Staff, instructor duty at Yale University, and being designated a Certified Public Accountant.

Ted Beal has been married to Gloria for sixty-five years; they have a son Kenneth and a daughter Cynthia, two grandchildren, and four great-grandchildren.

He is a member of the American Institute of CPA's, the Connecticut Society of CPAs and the Five Lakes Veterans Association.

The Messerschmitt BF-109E had 36,000 produced during WW II, the largest amount of Aircraft produced.

Joe E. Brown—traveled to visit the American troops over 150,000 miles.

The British 6th **Airborne** was nicknamed the "Red Devils."

Seven Hundred Journalists followed United States troops in all Theaters of the War—over four-hundred were at Normandy.

Medeiros, Richard M.	United States Navy
Water Tender-Combat Engineer	World War Two
10/1944-1946	USS Boxer CD-21

Rick, as all his friends know him down at the Reflections Roller Skating Rink, was born 10 February 1927 in Massachusetts and grew up in Newark, New Jersey, he had one younger brother, he told me that his mothers name was Alice, during the depression his father couldn't find work; that his uncle had a job in the coal yard where he sold coal in New York for 10 cents a bag, and he later developed lung problems from the coal dust.

Rick attended High School at South Side high, in Newark, NJ, he did remember some of the depression years, and said it was very rough.

While attending school, he played a lot of sports, baseball, basketball, football, etc. Some baseball games he remembers very clearly, it was the games that he played while playing on the YMCA team. They had lost the first game, after that he said that his team had won the next 20 games; something he will never forget.

Other than playing sports while attending school, Rick didn't like going to school much; one day he decided that he wasn't going to school, after his Mom sent him off that morning for school; he hid in the alley behind the houses. While he was there, a male stranger came by and ask him where the Medeiros lived, Rick sent him off on a wild-goose chase; where the man would have to climb three flight of stairs, then Rick ran out of the alley; he later learned that it was the school truant-officer because he hadn't been in school for several days.

Soon after that his parents signed papers so that he would be joining the military, he was only 17 years old; a war going on; it was 1944.

They signed him up during October of 1944; the United States was still at war with Germany and Japan. Rick took his Basic Training at Sampson Naval Base, New York, and after 8 weeks of basic training he graduated from basic; his mother and grandmother attended the graduation. From there he went on a shake down cruise; then to Cuba, after which they traveled back to Portmouth and were given a seven day leave.

He was transferred to Newport, Rhode Island Navy Base where he boarded a ship, the ship was torpedoed by the Japanese, at the time of the attack; he was in the boiler room. Richard said that they didn't have any life jackets and were in the water about six hours before being rescued.

Later Rick was assigned to the USS Boxer, CV-21 Aircraft Carrier; (Class: Ticonderoga, Displacement: 27100, Aircraft capacity 90-100, Fate: converted/reclassified) ; the USS Boxer ship was completed too late too take place in World War Two, it was commissioned in Portsmouth, Virginia, then they traveled to Annapolis where the ship was host for a new ship.

In 1945-46 she operated in the Western Pacific, visited Japan, Okinawa, the Philippines and China. After that they traveled to San Francisco, California to have guns mounted on the ship. Then they went to the South Pacific, the Panama Canal; for a while they were stuck in dry dock; after the war his ship took some important people to Alaska.

Richard was discharged in July 1946 after three years in the Pacific, during his military career he had earned the Victory Medal, Asiatic Pacific Medal, the American Theatre Medal and several Ribbons.

Today Rick is a frequent visitor at the Roller Skating Rink, where he spent many years skating; he also is a member of the Elks, VFW and Moose Organizations.

By May of 1945, World War Two had been going on for over three years and five months before the Germans surrendered, on 6 May 1945. The Atomic bomb was dropped on Hiroshima on 6 August 1945 and another atomic bombed dropped on Nagasaki on 9 August 1945. On 14 August Japan surrendered. On 2 September 1945 formal ceremonies on board battleship USS Missouri in Tokyo Bay took place.

United States Marine Corps

In the beginning the proposal to create the U.S. Marine Corps as an additional infantry regiment that would be used for sea service and shore duty "to defend the coast, work upon fortifications, or in dock yards, and guard the public property from thefts and embezzlement".

The role was varied over the years in response to current needs of the United States Government as well as changes in international law, politics and view points.

However, after their inception in 1798, the use of Marines expanded to include landings on foreign soil to protect the lives and property of American nationals living abroad, and to render able assistance to U.S. diplomatic representatives in establishing and maintaining foreign policies.

Those purposes were perhaps most clearly illustrated by the Corps throughout their history of service in China.

The following Veteran is one of those Marines that served in China.

Valcourt, Robert A. Sr.   United States Marine Corps
11/1944-11/1946   World War Two
                                     Occupied China

Veteran Bob Valcourt, was born 8 July 1927, in Brooklyn, New York and

raised and attended schools in Long Island, New York. While Bob was still in High School he volunteered for the draft. Because he had enough credits he was able to receive his high school diploma early.

On 20 September 1945 Bob and Vic his high school buddy, registered for the draft and chose the U.S. Marine Corps, Bob was transported to Paris Island, South Carolina for his basic training.

After completing his training, Bob was taken to Newport News, Virginia and placed on a ship that's destination was China; Bob said that he spent twenty-five days on the ship because the ship had to stop at different Islands located in the South Pacific including going through the Panama Canal to before arriving in China. From that time on until he was released from the military Bob was tagged a China Marine.

The China Marine

After World War Two, the Marines were sent to China to handle politically delicate circumstances; disarm and repatriate the defeated Japanese troops without taking sides in the brewing Chinese Civil War or engaging in conflict with the communist.

The 1st and 6th Marine Divisions of the III Amphibious Corps (IIIAC) were assigned to handle 500,000 defeated Japanese and civilians of the Hopeh Province and the Shantung Peninsula until Nationalist Government led by Chlanj Kai-shek could assume control of North China. The occupation of North China would prove to be both trying and dangerous.

One of the Marines proudest chapters of history is the duty in China assisting the Chinese in an attempt to repatriate defeated Japanese troops and restore peacetime life, the Marines conducted themselves in a manner which did their service and country proud and inspired loyalty in some Chinese citizens that is as strong today as it was sixty-eight years ago.

In November 1946, after spending one and one-half years in the 1st Marine Division, Bob was discharged with the rank of Pfc. and was awarded several medals and ribbons.

Bob met his wife Caroline in 1941 while in High School; they have two sons, Ronald & Robert. After his military service Bob went back to school to learn merchandising, an occupation that he continued until his retirement in 1990.

After his retirement Bob started roller skating when he was seventy-two years old, he skated at several Roller Skating Arena's in Florida. Bob now lives in Kissimmee, Florida with his beautiful wife Caroline.

Rosie the Riveter—While women worked in a variety of positions previously closed to them, the aviation industry saw the greatest increase in female workers. More than 310,000 women worked in the U.S. Aircraft industry in 1943, representing 65 percent of the industry's total workforce (compared to just 1 percent in the pre-war years). The munitions industry also heavily recruited women workers, as represented by the U.S. governments "Rosie the Riveter" propaganda campaign. Based in small part on a real-life munitions worker, but primarily a fictitious character, the strong, bandanna-clad Rosie became one of the most successful recruitment tools in American history, and the most iconic image of working women. wikipedia.org

Women in the Armed Forces—In addition to factory work and other home front jobs, some 350,000 women joined the Armed Services, serving at home and abroad. At the urging of First Lady Eleanor Roosevelt and women's groups, and impressed by the British use of women in service, General George Marshall supported the idea of introducing a women service branch into the Army. In May 1942, Congress instituted the Women's Auxiliary Army Corps, later upgraded to the Women's Army Corps, which had full military status. Its members, known as WACs, worked in more than 200 non-combatant jobs stateside and in every theater of the war. By 1945, there were more than 100,000 WACs and 6,000 female officers. In the Navy members of Women accepted for Volunteer Emergency Service (WAVES) held the same status as naval reservists and provided support stateside. The Coast Guard and Marine Corps soon followed suit, though in smaller numbers.

The following Female Veteran served during the years following World War Two.

Harwell (Welden) Elizabeth A.
United States Air Force
Sergeant, Clerical Typist
Served in Country
11/1948-07/1950

Our next American veteran, being a female and joining the United States Armed Forces less than three years after World War Two ended took a great deal of courage for this young beauty. She was all of twenty years old, born 17 August 1928, in a suburb of Philadelphia, called Ridley Park.

Betty decided that she wanted to do something for her country and if the next part of the story was up to a screen play writer, he might have gone to the nearest Air Force recruiter and sailed into the wild blue yonder. But not this young lady, she had heard so many stories of what the U.S. Soldiers and Sailors had done while fighting for our America freedom that she was willing to help also, so she enlisted in the U.S. Air Force.

There had been other members of her family that served in the U.S. Armed Forces, her father, Curtin Welden (now deceased), served with the U.S. Army in occupied Germany after World War Two ended. Her uncle Raymond Welden, was in the Army during World War One; in Germany, he lost a leg due to being gassed. Betty's brother Curtin D. Welden, a WW II and Korean Veteran, served in the U.S. Navy and his son Curtin D. Weldin, Jr. was a peacetime Navy Veteran.

After Betty passed her written and physical exams, she was assigned and transported to Lackland Air Force Base, San Antonio, Texas, to muster in with the rest of the lassies and learn the basics. Betty was assigned to the 3742nd WAF Squadron (2nd WAF Sq.). Betty's roommate, Terry Jordan enlisted the same day in Philadelphia, their room was in an old World War

Two, two-story wooden barracks, and it was a plywood cubicle with two Army cots, a wooden shelf to store items on; with a broom handle attached underneath to hang clothes on, two foot lockers,

On Friday evening, Terry wanted to go to the movies with a few friends; Betty said she was staying in to clean the room for Saturday morning inspection. After washing the linoleum floor, Betty found some "glass wax" from the supply room, and put it all over the floor; when she finished at the doorway, a WFA came by and asked what she was using on the floor? Betty said, "Glass wax" so it will make the floor shine. The WAF, let out a big laugh and said, it's for windows, not floors, needless to say, Betty had to wash the linoleum over again. Betty was still washing the floor when her room mate returned for the evening and was surprised to find Betty still cleaning the room. Terry laughed, and said we are going to need a flash light to finish, its ten o'clock and lights out, the next morning the room did pass inspection.

After completing basic training, Betty and Terry were sent to Clerk-Typist School in the 3450th Technical Training Wing at Francis E. Warren AFB, Cheyenne, Wyoming. Betty was an "Honor Student" in her typing class and won the privilege of choosing what base she wanted to transfer to. She selected Barksdale, as Terry was transferring there. (Terry is now in a nursing home in Florida, and Betty has visited her there.)

At Barksdale AFB, Betty teamed up with the 3500th Pilot Training Wing, AFB, (Bossier City). Betty also served with the 3500th WAF Squadron, and the 3605th Navigator Training Wing, Ellington AFB, Houston, Texas. Her assignments were typing for Technical and Legal Offices at Barksdale and Ellington Air Force Bases. Betty said that she never handled any weapons; she left that up to the G.I.'s.

Betty met her future husband Cicero G. (Lucky) Harwell while being assigned to the base legal office; he was a typing instructor and Dewey Decimal system teacher. In June 1950 Betty married Sgt. Cicero G. (Lucky)

Harwell. After serving in the United States Air Force for one year and eight months, Betty was discharged in July 1950 at Ellington Air Force Base, Houston, Texas.

Returning to civilian life she joined her husband, then stationed at Reese Air Force Base, in Lubbock, Texas. After her discharge Betty continued working doing clerical and civilian typing on different bases in country; wherever her husband was stationed. By the time her husband was discharged in 1970 he had achieved the rank of Senior Master Sergeant.

Betty and Lucky Harwell had two children, Linda Ann and Thomas have three grandsons, two grand-daughters and one great-grandson. Unfortunately, Senior Master Sergeant Harwell passed away in October 2005 in Winter Haven, Florida. Lucky is featured in the last chapter of this book along with other deceased veterans.

Betty is now living in Lake Alfred, Florida, where she keeps busy with several organizations and clubs; she is a member of the Ladies Auxiliary of Auburndale FL.; VFW Post 4945, where she serves on several committees. She enjoys going to yard sales, looking for Betty Boop items among other items. Betty also enjoys doing crossword puzzles, cryptograms, e-mailing relatives and friends, researching genealogy of family members, making nylon net scrubbie's and reading.

Betty said that one of the highlights of her military career, was when she was at basic training, her squadron went to Washington, D.C. in January 1949 to march in President Harry Truman's Inaugural Parade, and that her Squadron was the "Honor Guard" when Bob Hope and his entertainers, Jerry Colonna, Doris Day, Irene Ryan (who later played Granny in "The Beverly Hillbillies" TV show), and Les Brown and his Band of Renown put on a fabulous show for Lackland Air Force Base.

She also mentioned that meeting her husband, Lucky, at Lackland was fate and they were married for fifty-five years before his passing. Proving that Yankees and Rebels can get along! (Lucky was from Arkansas).

The Korean War—In August 1945, Korea was separated, and an artificial boundary between the communist-controlled North and the South was established at the 38th parallel. Almost five years later, on Sunday, 25 June 1950, armored and infantry units of the North Korean Army crossed the boarder in a full-scale invasion of the South. These events were invasions, preceded in earnest to conquer and enslave the natives of their country. The natives were helpless against the attacks of their Northern neighbors.

Korea—Chosin Reservoir between 27 November and around the middle December 1950; the day after thanksgiving the U.N. troops were getting into position around the Chosin reservoir, the freezing-point was dropping steadily, it was about twenty degrees below freezing, and everything was turning to ice.

A notorious seventeen day and night battle followed between about 30,000 United Nations troops and the 67,000 Chinese troops that had surrounded the U.N. troops at the Chosin Reservoir. After days and nights of cold and brutal fighting, the Marines formed into a convoy with a single M4A3 Sherman tank at the front.

On 1 December, the 3rd Battalion, 7th Marines engaged the PVA 175th Regiment of the 59th Division at Hill 1542 and Hill 1419, unfortunately, the Chinese garrison drove the Marines back and they had to dig in on the icy slopes. Besides the troops on Hill 1542 and 1492, there were on the other three sides of the entrapment United Nation troops trying to break through. All though the Chinese troops outnumbered the UN forces, the United Nation forces broke out of the siege. The evacuation of the X-Corps from the port of Hungnam marked the complete withdrawal of UN troops from the North Koreans at the Frozen Chosin, December 1950.

Thirteen Congressional Medals' of Honor were awarded to individual troops that fought at the Chosin Reservoir campaign.

In Korea on 25 October 1951, the truce talks resumed. The fighting continued until 27 July 1953, when both sides finally agreed to a truce. However, some small battles continued even after the truce.

Lamping, Robert S. Cpl
United States Army
65th Combat Engineer03/1943-03/1946 s
25thInfantry Division
C Company—Japan Korea
1948-1952

Robert was born on Flag Day, June 14, 1931, in Rogers Park Hospital the far northeast side of Chicago. He is the oldest of 10, six sisters and three brothers. Graduated from Harriet Beecher Stowe Grammar School, and then went to Lane Technical High school. After graduating from High School he went to Wright Junior College for one year.

Robert enlisted into the US Army on 18 November 1948, at Camp Breckinridge, KY and did his basic training with the 101st Airborne Infantry Division. After accomplishing his training, he was given a thirty—day—furlough to visit his parents.

After his 30 day furlough Robert was told to report to a replacement depot in Seattle, Washington. From Seattle he went across the Pacific Ocean aboard an Army Troop Ship called the "General Briggs" to Tokyo Japan. Then he traveled by rail to Osaka, Japan, (the third largest city in the world at the time) and he was assigned to the 65th Combat Engineer Battalion, 25th Infantry Division, AP025 for Japan peace time occupation (under General MacArthur's command), until June of 1950.

Then the North Koreans crossed the 38th Parallel invading South Korea, Robert along with other troops was immediately confined to the camp at "Kanoaka Barracks; as it was called. They proceeded to be shipped out by rail to Sasabo, Japan debarkation depot. Also the jeeps, trucks, tanks, and other equipment were loaded aboard ships sailing from Sasabo, Japan to Pusan, South Korea.

Aboard ship they were told to keep a lookout for enemy submarine periscopes. It was a nighttime crossing. Needless to say, everyone was afraid of being torpedoed. Once they arrived in Pusan; all ranks were frozen. They immediately started driving the vehicles and transporting the men, weapons, ammunition and supplies to the front lines.

While serving in Korea, Robert visited a few settlements ; Kaesan, Inchon, Yong Dong Po, Soul, and they rowed the infantry across the Han River under heavy enemy fire, it took them two nights and two days without any rest.

After capturing Soul, Robert's group advanced to the Yalu River, which is the border line that separates China from North Korea. After digging along the Yalu River, the Chinese army crossed over and proceeded to push them back all the way to the Mason (Pusan) front. There, the 25th Division had its backs to the water and was told there is nowhere to go. And they were ordered to fight to the last man. (Below is a short scenario of the Pusan Perimeter Campaign).

It was then that reinforcement troops started arriving, and when the Marines cut off the enemies supply lines at the Inchon landing, they started to "kick butt" and started retreating back to the 38th Parallel. There, they held the line under General Ridgeway's command, while negotiations for peace were being attempted.

Robert said that it would take him forever to give all the details of his stay in the Korean War, so to sum it up, he had accumulated enough points to be shipped back to the United States in June, 1951. For his military service; Robert was awarded the National Defense Service Medal, Korean Service Medal with one silver and one bronze service star, the United Nations Medal, Army of Occupation Medal with Japan clasp, Republic of Korea Presidential Unit Citation Badge, Good Conduct Medal, Marksman Badge with Rifle Bar and retaining the rank of Corporal.

He was shipped back to Tokyo, Japan and from Tokyo was transported back to the United States aboard an Army Troop ship, the "General Meigs". The ship embarked at Camp Stoneman, California and from there Corporal Robert S. Lamping flew home to Chicago; and he stayed with his parents for his thirty-day furlough before reporting to Camp McCoy (now Fort McCoy) Wisconsin.

At Camp McCoy Robert was ordered by President Truman to serve for a one year extension because of the unsettled situation concerning the Korean War. He was finally discharged at Fort Sheridan, Illinois on 23 June 1952.

Robert is the brother of Bill and Joseph Lamping, also featured in this book.

Pusan Perimeter—A retreat of Pusan would result in one of the greatest butcheries in history. We must fight to the end. We must fight as a team. If some of us die, we will die fighting together, Maj. Gen. Walton Walker said in a desperate bid to rally his forces. During the heat of the summer 1950 Walker had 47,000 U.S. troops from the 24th, 25th and 1st Cavalry Divisions on the western length of the Pusan perimeter. The United Nations force had to cling to a toehold that was hardly more than an expanded beachhead. The fighting was necessary to defend the Pusan perimeter a small strip of land at the lower end of the peninsula protecting the only port and airfield the Americans had left where they could land reinforcements and supplies. The land ran along the last remaining natural barrier before the sea, the Naktong River.

An essential trick of survival was learning to fight from all sides of a foxhole, front, back, left and right, as the North Koreans exhausted themselves in their all out fury, and everyone was told help was on the way. The communists were just 33 air miles from Pusan, pushing forward with 7,500 men, 36 artillery tubes and 25 tanks.

The counterthrust began 7 August with the 35th Regiment of the 25th Division. The counterattack stopped in its tracks. The Americans controlled the roads, but the North Koreans controlled the countryside. It would take dirty fighting to flush them off the hills. A place called Battle Mountain changed hands 19 times, sometimes two of three times in a single day. Finally by the morning of 19 August, Marines and soldiers linked up at the river. (reference to the Navy Times).

Pennella, Angelo
United States Army
19th Ordinance—8th Army
Korean War
09/1952-09/1954

Newark, New Jersey, a town west of New York City, in the early 1930's was just beginning to grow and on 22 February 1932 the population was increased by at least one more male; Angie as we like to call him at the skating rink, came into the world after the depression and when he was just nine years old the United States had been attacked by the Japanese. Angie, in grade school at the time; didn't have to grow up alone, he had a younger brother Anthony, he has passed on.

Although Anthony is no longer with us in person, he is remembered everyday of Angie's life, he was here with Angie growing up, they attended St. Ann's School together, they entered the military at the same time and later on in life they ran a food business together.

September, 1952, during the height of the Korean War Angie was drafted into the United States Army, although he was told by his many friends to join the National Guard, (they would say, "if you join the Guard, you won't have to go to Korea"). Much to Angie's regret, he didn't join the National Guard; and so he was drafted into the US Army. Angie was shipped to Camp Kilmer New Jersey. He told me that it was the worst time of his life, when he arrived there, he was told that he had kitchen duty. That's when it finally hit him and he felt all alone, Angie was starting to ask himself why didn't I listen to those guys, he sat down in a corner of the pantry and actually started crying; he felt so alone.

Soon the head chef in charge of the kitchen came in and saw him. He said to Angie, so you don't like it here? I'll fix you so you can have real tears and he gave Angie a whole bucket of onions to peel and left the kitchen. Angie looking around and noticed a large machine for peeling potatoes, he dumped the onions into it and turned the machine on, the onions, he said; came out like little balls. When the head chef returned to the kitchen he was furious, he told Angie wait until tomorrow, I'll really give you a job you can handle. Lucky for Angie the next day his Unit was shipped out.

He was sent to Aberdeen, Maryland for Basic training. After completing basic, Angie was placed into the 19th Ordinance Unit, which is where he spent the rest of his two year hitch. The Ordinance Unit takes care of all the heavy mobile equipment, moving it and repairing it. Angie told me that when he first arrived in Korea, they were using equipment that was left over from World War Two.

After Basic Training was completed, he went home for a few days leave before being shipped to South Korea. During the few days he was home, his mother gave him a rosary necklace and told him to carry it all the time, that way he would never be alone. He did, he wore it while serving in Korea and still wears them today. When he went back on duty, Angie was shipped from Maryland to California, where he was loaded on a troop ship along with 4,000 other troops. Like so many of his shipmates, he was seasick the whole time. The ship stopped in Okinawa before hitting the Port of Korea.

Angie said that when they arrived in Korea, it was like no mans land, the Korean War had been going on for two years now and most of the buildings were bombed out, their was no trees, all the bridges were blown up, the people had nothing; the natives made and lived in mud huts, it was very depressing, whenever the natives could; they would steal. Where he was stationed was called Chin Chon.

Angie had a couple of the young boys working for him, as did many of the other troops.

Brother Anthony Pennella was also drafted right out of the Washington Senators Baseball Team; but he played Baseball for the United States Army all during his military tour of duty. He was a catcher.

Angelo Pennella was discharged in September of 1954; he married Elizabeth (Betty) on January 9, 1955 (they have been married 58 years). They had two children, one boy and one girl and five grandchildren.

Angie and his brother Anthony started their business together soon after being discharged from the military. First they worked in Industrial Catering and later had their own business with Stewarts Root Beer, in Tuckerton, New Jersey. While interviewing he said that he misses his brother Anthony everyday.

Angie Pennella is retired now, still lives in Little Egg Harbor, New Jersey during the warmer months and spends the winter months in Florida. He is an advent roller skater and we get to join him skating every Wednesday during the winter at Skate Reflections in Kissimmee, Florida

MacCrea, Richard S.   United States Army
Signal Core
01/23/1952-08/1952   San Luis, Obispo, CA

Richard MacCrea was born 23 March 1931, in a small town named Glen Ridge, New Jersey, he also grew up and attended schools in Glen Ridge. Richard attended school behind his sister Marie, and she was seven years older than him. Richard recalled that his favorite teacher's name was Ms. Peas, and while attending the 8th grade; he learned a great deal about grammar in her classroom.

Glen Ridge traces its beginning to 1666 when Connecticut families led by Robert Trent bought land from the Lenni Lenape Native Americans and named it New Ark to reflect a covenant to worship freely without persecution. Glen Ridge was a section composed mostly of farms and woodlands with the exception of a thriving industrial area along the Toney's Brook in the Glen. Some notable former and current residents of Glen Ridge include: Buzz Aldrin, Apollo 11 crew, Horace Ashenfelter, Olympic gold medalist, Kerry Berra, son of Yogi Berra, Tom Cruise, graduated from Glen Ridge High School, Gary Cuozzo, NFL player and many more.

During the summer months Richard, his sister, mom and grandmother enjoyed the MacCrea summer home at the Point Pleasant, New Jersey Sea Shore and his father would join them on weekends. One summer he remembered very clearly is when it rained for seventeen days straight; he said that summer his grandmother had a stroke at the shore and because of the rain Richard ended up very sick.

The story went like this; his two playmates wanted to ride bicycles to Bay Head a beach resort; while Richard rode along with them it started raining and when they reached the beach Richard did not have on a bathing suit under his clothes; the other two boys did and they jumped in the water.

So Richard rode home in the rain and was soaked when he arrived, and he ended up with pneumonia, then it turned into TB; which left him with severe allergies.

Richard also did a lot of roller skating in the streets, but his biggest interest was tinkering with radios and cars. He had earned a quarter a week allowance from his father, and he saved every bit of it. After saving enough money to purchase a broken radio from the local radio thrift store he would take it home and repair it.

Richard learned how to fix a lot of radios, so many that the store owner offered him a job working in his store fixing peoples broken radios when he was thirteen to fourteen. In 1948 when the first television's came out, Richard also soon learned how to fix them.

After graduating from high school Richard found full time employment at General Instruments. They manufactured record changers and TV Tuners. He was a technician in the department that designed and built test and calibration equipment for TV Tuners Production.

From General Instruments he went to a company much closer to home. This company manufactured hand walkie—talkies for the military. He was responsible for maintaining and calibrating all production test equipment, he worked here until he was drafted. All this knowledge would later prove to pay off when he joined the military.

During the Korean War Richard joined up on January 23, 1952. During his initial interview for the Army, the recruiters learned that Richard was experienced in electronics; they signed him up for the Southwest Signal Corps Training Center.

Richard was flown out of New Jersey in a DC-6 and taken to Camp San Luis Obispo, CA the original home of the California Army National Guard. Because the facility had not been used for quite a long time the grass had grown quite high. At the time that Richard was stationed there the base was just going through a rehab, Richard's first assignment was to help cut down the tall grass.

Camp San Luis Obispo, formerly called Camp Merriam, was established in 1928 and is called the original home of the California National Guard. It served as an infantry Division Camp and Cantonment Area for the United States Army during World War II. The camp is in San Luis Obispo County, which is on the Central Coast of California. During World War II, the camp had quarters for 1,523 officers and 19,383 enlisted personnel.

Following the outbreak of hostilities in Korea in 1950, mobilization of the 40th Infantry Division and several support units of the California National Guard; the Army again leased Camp San Luis Obispo as a Class 1 installation. The Southwest Signal Corps Training Center was located at the camp as a Class II activity.

It was at this facility; Richards first duty station, that he had taken sick due to the allergic reaction from cutting grass and weeds, and he had asthma attacks as his unit was preparing the field for military aircraft. He landed in the hospital twice and it was the US Army's decision that he was unable to perform any duties with his medical condition and he was medically discharged after six months, he received his discharge papers in August 1952.

After being discharged Richard did however continue his work and interest in the electronic field and secured a position with Stavid Engineering working on radar equipment. During this period Richard broadened his skills in skating and was a regular at the Roller Skating Rink in Paramus, New Jersey where he met his wife Virginia; they were married 30 April 1959.

From Stavid Engineering, Richard went to Chatham Electronics, then to New Jersey Electronic. He worked his way up from technician to Project Engineer. After a time he went to work for Heyer Industries designing automotive test equipment. He found a position that involved his two interests Car's and electronics.

He said this was not a job, this to him was fun. He was promoted to the position of Senior Project Engineer. Heyer was acquired by Marquette Corp and in 1963 moved engineering from Belleville, NJ to Minneapolis, MN. Richard said he didn't mind the cold then, he enjoyed snowmobiling but the pollution in the summer time was too much and in 1972 he accepted an offer from JLB Consultants in Winter Haven, FL.

The position did not involve cars and electronics, but the pay was good and he had no problem with pollen. In 1984 Richard was offered the job of Service Manager for the State of Florida for Bear Automotive, formally Marquette Corp, and that was the job from which he retired.

Richard's sister Marie volunteered for the United States Marines during World War Two, she served as a Chaplains Assistant. Richard told me that she passed in 2004.

Long before Richard retired his parents and sister moved to Florida, Richard and his wife moved to Florida in 1972. Richard and his wife Virginia had three daughters and one son, and have ten grandchildren plus great-grandchildren.

The Korean War ultimately involved 22 countries and left Korea a ravaged, smoking ruin that stank of death. More than 4 million men, women and children were killed, wounded or otherwise incapacitated in the war, including 2 million civilians in North and South Korea. Truman's police action left 54,246 Americans dead, including 33,629 in combat and 20,617 killed from accidents or illness. There were also 103,284 Americans wounded.

Angello, Joseph J.

BUC (SCW) (AA)
NMCB-133,12,13&14
1954-58, 1960-64,
1983-2000

US Air Force, US Navy &
USNR
Navy Seabees
Grenada—Panama

Urgent Fury—Just Cause

Born 1 October 1937, in Carbondale, Pennsylvania, Joe grew up in Pennsylvania and New York; Joe attended Manhattan High School of Aviation Trades and Columbia University. He enlisted into the Air Force at age seventeen years, took his Basic Training at Sampson Air Force Base, Geneva, New York. After completing his training he was assigned to the 331st Fighter Interceptor Squadron

While serving in the United States Air Force stationed in the Eastern Air Defender Command (ADC), some of Joe's responsibilities were that of Aircraft Instruments, Auto Pilot as an E-5

After being discharged from the Air Force in 1958, Joe married in April 1959; he soon became dissatisfied with civilian life and enlisted in the USN as an E-3, Signalman (SM). He was honorably discharged in March 1964, an E-5 (SM2). For the next eighteen years in his own words, he struggled to support his wife and three children.

During that period he had several occupations, he drove a Greyhound Bus for ten years before starting his own construction company in New Jersey. He had the opportunity to advance his education by becoming a police officer in New York City. Having his tuition to Columbia University paid for over five years; Joe left NYC and NYDP to take a position as a Field Engineer for a labor construction company in Syracuse, NY.

1983-2000 US Navy Seabees

In Joe's own words, Joe said that while working at Fort Drum, NY, I witnessed a Seabee detachment at work. I soon had committed myself to work into the Seabees. I read all I could find on them and had many conversations with their members. January 1983, I reenlisted into the Seabees Reserves, which was at the time R-NMCB-12 as an E-5 (BU2) and was almost immediately activated in April 83 and assigned to the 2nd Marine Division. M.E.U. (Marine Expeditionary Unit) and soon after was on my way to Grenada (Urgent Fury).

Returning to the US, I found that the "R" in Reserves was eliminated from Reserve Seabee Battalion. A new presidential order had made all Seabee reservists subject to recall by the President; without the approval of Congress. This opened up vast world wide deployments for the Bees. I became a member of the 12th Battalion's Air Detachment, (a self contained, air mobile construction unit). I was assigned as their Air Det. Military Instructor and sent to Camp Pendleton, CA for Marine military tactics and advanced weapons training.

Upon graduation from the Marine Instructors School, I became the Senior Military Instructor for the 12th Battalion's Air Detachment (E-6). Our leadership (CO) acquired joint service tasking with Air Force Command at Otis AFB in Cape Cod, MA. Monthly the air detachment mounted out in C-130 from Glen Falls and Albany, NY, to Otis AFB and AF projects and training.

In the second year of these evolutions our project accomplishments for the Air Force; our training caught the attention of the upper military brass of the Air Force, Army and even the Navy. Notably during a planned Seabee exercise called (Green Stinger), in this exercise a fully loaded C5A aircraft suddenly approached and landed at Otis AFB in the pre dawn hours and disgorged a fully equipped air detachment.

Heavy trucks and equipment spilled out of the giant aircraft, loaded with armed and painted (Seabee) Commandos, who quickly secured the runway and all access areas. Unknown to the base personnel, the operation was approved by the Base Commander. The Air Force Personal did not have any idea of what was happening, but quickly understood that they were captured and offered no resistance to the heavily armed Bees.

Although the entire exercise was monitored and witnessed by high ranking Air Force and Navy command, the operation was supposed to be secret; however, the size of the C5A loading at Quonset Point, Road Island prior to take-off had attracted the local media complete with TV cameras and crew. The exercise came off in such a spectacular way that plans for the Air Detachment would be studied and enhanced by the powers that existed at the time.

1985-6 Entered problems in Central America: Our Air Detachment leaders at the time proved the flexibility and economy of utilizing the Naval Seabee Air Detachment as fast response unit readily available to answer limited emergencies almost anywhere in the world (we were subject to re-call and mount out in 72 hours).

Although our C130 Aircraft could land or take off from limited undeveloped fields they had very little security for our Air Craft arrival and defense.

In response, the advanced party concept (long in CB opps.); the Air Assault teams were formed and we received our training at Fort Benning, GA. We completed our training just in time to participate in the operation called "Just Cause" (Dec. 89).

In the pre dawn arrival from the sea, we were able to neutralize the Panamanian Defense Force PDF-(there was little opposition) base at Fort Amador before dawn. Our teams performed admirably but bad news awaited us upon our return to the US. Back in Davisville, RI, we learned that our beloved 12th Battalion was to be retired, after serving honorably through WW II, Korea, Vietnam, Grenada and Panama.

Promoted to CPO 1989.

 1992-94 transferred to NMCB-13, at Watertown, NY Reserve Center I was assigned OIC (and officer available to travel that far north) for the 84 man Delta Company, NMCB-13 was also slated for decommissioning, so my time there was limited. D Company as I was assigned was a remnant of the retired 21st Regiment; hence, "I had charge of 84 teachers".

In an effort to instill Seabee discipline and being virtually unknown by my new units, I continued to push my small unit to be proficient in actual military training. I moved the unit to New Quarters at Fort Drum, NY. The 10th Mountain Division had more than enough projects to keep my Seabees busy. Our CM & EO Personal paid our rent by lending their services to their ECS (Equipment Concentration Site), they trained and were trained in support of the most modern military equipment anywhere.

Through civilian & military contacts I was able to learn of a two story (old) wooden barracks that our men rehabbed and made livable; total cost to me $1.00 per year. I was also lucky in meeting the man who was in charge of the forts DROM, a place where condemned or worn out military equipment was put up for sale (bid). Here I bought a 2 and ½ ton truck for $1.00 that the CM's built with parts and tires from the Army. Now, complete with our Seabee logo properly stenciled on the doors; our unit sported our own transport (on base only) and we even arranged for the Army to pay for the fuel we used.

One notable accomplishment achieved while in NMCB-13, I was charged by Battalion with the construction of a new Air Assault School at Camp Smith in Peekskill, NY for the US Military Academy at West Point. Having the responsibility to man the project, I was fortunate in acquiring the yearly best talent from my old 12th Battalion buddies, as well as the best Petty Officers from my own small unit.

Together, we were able to construct the best assault training facility in the country with the (at the time) tallest assault tower (60ft.) and two assault ramps in record time; during the winter. Upon completion, the grand opening was witnessed by some of the highest brass in the country (Army & Navy), everyone shaking hands and patting each others back in celebration of their newest facility.

I myself missed the celebration of the grand opening due to other assignments (not even an Atta boy); from the Navy or NMCB-13. "Many good works go unrecognized by our respective commands".

1994: Personal tragedy took my home by fire in January 94, my new wife; Honeybee Anna and I elected to start over in a far warmer place. I was transferred to NMCB-14 in Jacksonville, FL and assigned to trouble shoot the leadership of their Tampa Detachment (C.C.O.) upon arrival at the Tampa Reserve Center; I studied what was a much unorganized operation.

The station Commander was in the habit of using Seabees to perform basic maintenance on his Reserve Center, and allowing limited time and space for Seabee training. Knowing Seabees did not belong in a Reserve center, I took it upon myself to relocate this unit out of the reach of the Reserve Center Command, knowing full well the position and responsibility of the Reserve Center Command, as well as the Naval Construction Force Command structure.

After a most agreeably meeting with the Reserve Center C.O., I was able to point out successfully the difference in the chain of command of the Fleet vs the NCF and the need for Seabees to train at a military installation where proper training was available.

A successful meeting with the C.O. at the 6th Refueling Sq (a great guy), we were given office space and training facilities at Mac Dill A.F.B.

Throughout my service with NMCB-14, I remained Charlie Company Chief and Military Advisor to S-2 Shop for Seabee Military Training, sharing my experiences and knowledge when needed. I retired from NMCB-14 in August of 2000, at the age of 63 years. I had and enjoyed many titles, and wore many hats over the years, but the one of which I am most proud was teacher.

During the past 46 years or so, I have had many, many experiences. Experiences I will cherish for the rest of my days were those years with the US Navy Seabee. Signed, Joe

Joe continues to be active now that he is retired; at the present time he is Commander of Island X-2, NSVA (Navy Seabees Veterans of America), Lakeland, Florida and resides with his beautiful wife, Honeybee Anna in Zephyrhills, Florida.

Lamping, Joseph R.	United States Army
Field Artillery	101st Air Borne
08/1958-08/1960	Missouri, Kentucky

Joe was born 22 October 1935, he grew up and attended schools in Illinois, when he turned twenty-two years old, he volunteered for U.S. Military Service, on 22 August 1958.

He attended Air Borne School in Fort Campbell, Kentucky, after finishing all his training and testing, Joe was assigned to the 2nd Airborne Battle Group, 187th Infantry.

After serving in the military for two years, Joe was honorably discharged; he was awarded several Medals and Ribbons for his military service.

Returning to civilian life, he obtained the employment as a butcher; he now lives with his wife in Leesburg, Florida, and together they have one son.

Lamping, William United States Army
Military Truck Driver Korean Era
Nov. 1958-Nov. 1960 54th Infantry-Germany

Bill was born April 1940 in Chicago, IL and grew up in Chicago and Palatine, Illinois; he was the fifth child of his parents ten children, they also adopted two more. His earliest incidents that sticks with him today was that he and two of his brothers were taking a walk when the two brothers while; horsing around, left Billy standing between two street-cars and started running away, Bill was 5 or 6 years old at the time. During grade school, his favorite time was playing sports and that his favorite teacher was Ms. Davis, his 6th grade teacher.

While he was a young lad growing up Bill worked around his Uncle Frank's Dairy Farm in Union Grove, Wisconsin, he recalled that his grandmother had a garden in front of her house at the farm and he enjoyed picking the strawberries in it; although she would get mad. It was also his job to feed the chickens; once while clowning around he had hid the kettle for feeding them, his uncle was so mad that he made him clean out the chicken coop. Another time he was driving the tractor and it tipped over, the two wagons that he was pulling tipped over also; fortunately he didn't get hurt.

When Bill was old enough to venture out on his own, he found a skating rink in Arlington Heights, IL. Early on Bill knew that he wanted to learn how to skate; he would go to the rink and peek through the building to watch the skaters. One day the owner by the name of Madeline gave him a pair of skates; he said because she felt sorry for him. And that was the beginning of Bills never ending skating days.

When he was a skater at the Roller Arena in Wheaton, IL at 16 years old he first met his wife Jean of 53 years. She told me that she was only 13 years old at that time but knew at first sight that Bill Lamping was the boy she wanted to marry; Bill said that he rode his bicycle to meet her while they first starting dating.

Bill Lamping was eighteen years old on November 24, 1958 when he volunteered for United States Military Service. He enlisted in Des Plaines, Illinois, and did his Basic Training at Fort Leavenworth, MO. Bill was shipped to Ft Hood Texas after completing his basic training, he said, while at that facility, you weren't suppose to have street clothes there, but he was able to sneak them in and he would sneak out to the local skating rink.

Also when he was stationed at Ft. Hood, he had a Mohawk hair cut and it wasn't against regulations. Jean was only 15 before Bill was given orders for his transfer to Germany. With her parents permission she was allowed to take the train and visit Bill before he was shipped out to, Germany.

 Bill traveled to Germany by ship, the USS Upshur; (a merchant ship). He told me that the people in Germany were very friendly, they would take him places; such as the Black Forest, to Paris, to see the Eifel Tower, he said you could drive to Paris; that it was very close to the German border. Bill also took his roller skates to Germany, and yes, he found a roller skating rink, it was an outside rink with live music.

Bills Military Occupation (M.O.) while serving was that of a military vehicle (truck) driver, he said that he didn't have a whole lot to do because he served during peacetime. Bill also stated that he didn't receive a weapon until about 5 or 6 months after arriving in Germany; he was issued an M-1 rifle.

Bill completed his military service and was discharged November 24, 1960. He told me that he experienced that American people were grateful for his military service and treated him with many thanks; also treated him to food and drink items wherever he went. He said that his military experience made him a better person.

Arriving back in civilian life he was given the job back that he left behind when he joined the military. Bill Lamping worked for National Tea, later he worked for the 5th School District, and he started as custodian and finished as maintenance manager. He married his long time sweetheart in 1961; they had and raised three children, Betty, Billy and Allen, they have fourteen grandchildren and nine great-grandchildren.

Bill and Jean Lamping still roller skate, usually at Reflections Rink in Kissimmee, Florida. Bill is also an antique car buff; He said the high point of his life is being married to Jean.

The Cuban Missile Crisis—known as the October crisis in Cuba and the Caribbean Crisis, was a 13 day confrontation in October 1962 between the Soviet Union and Cuba on one side and the United States on the other side. It was one of the major confrontations of the Cold War, and is generally regarded as the moment in which the Cold War came closest to turning into a nuclear conflict. It is also the first documented instance of the threat of mutual assured destruction being discussed as a determining factor in a major international arms agreement.

After the U.S. had placed nuclear missiles in Turkey, aimed at Moscow, and the failed U.S. attempt to overthrow the Cuban regime (Bay of Pigs, Operation Mongoose), in May 1962, Nikita Khrushchev proposed the idea of placing Soviet nuclear missiles in Cuba to deter any future invasion attempt.

During a meeting between Khrushchev and Fidel Castro that July, a secret agreement was reached and construction of several missile sites began in the late summer. Such a move would also neutralize the U.S.'s advantage of having missiles in Turkey. These preparations were noticed and on 14 October, a U.S. U-2 aircraft took several pictures clearly showing sites for medium-range and intermediate-range ballistic nuclear missiles under construction. These images were processed and presented on 15 October, which marks the beginning of the 13-day crisis from the U.S. perspective.

The United States considered attacking Cuba via air and sea, but decided on a military blockade instead, calling it "quarantine" for legal and other reasons.

The U.S. announced that it would not permit offensive weapons to be delivered to Cuba, demanded that the Soviets dismantle the missile bases already under construction or completed, and return all offensive weapons to the USSR. The Kennedy administration held a slim hope that the Kremlin would agree to their demands, and expected a military confrontation.

On the Soviet side, Premier Nikita Khrushchev wrote in a letter from 24 October 1962, to President John F. Kennedy, that his blockade of navigation in international waters and air space constituted an act of aggression, propelling human kind into the abyss of a world nuclear-missile war.

However, in secret back-channel communications the President and Premier initiated a proposal to resolve the crisis. While this was taking place, several Soviet ships attempted to run the blockade, increasing tensions to the point that orders were sent out to U.S Navy ships to fire warning shots and then open fire.

On 27 October, a U-2 plane was shot down by a Soviet missile crew, and action that could have resulted in immediate retaliation from the Kennedy crisis cabinet, according to Secretary of Defense McNamara's later testimony. Kennedy stayed his hand and the negotiations continued.

The confrontation ended on 28 October 1962, when Kennedy and United Nations Secretary-General U Thant reached an agreement with

Khrushchev. Publicly, the Soviets would dismantle their offensive weapons in Cuba and return them to the Soviet Union, subject to United Nations verification, in exchange for a U.S. public declaration and agreement never to invade Cuba.

Secretly, the U.S. also agreed that it would dismantle all U.S. built Jupiter IRBMs, armed with nuclear warheads, which were deployed in Turkey and Italy against the Soviet Union.

After the removal of the missiles and Ilyushin II-28 light bombers from Cuba, the blockade was formally ended at 6:45 PM EST on 20 November 1962.(ref.militry-the press of freedom)

Smith, Donald R. CWO4	United States Navy
Gunners Mate	Cuba Crisis, Vietnam
Surface Ordinance Tech.	Japan, Vietnam Campaign
07/1959-02/1990	

Naval veteran Donald Smith is certainly no stranger to the United States Navy, having spent almost half his life in its service, Donald was born on 1 August 1941 in Weston, West Virginia. Some of his earliest memories are stories about his great-grandfather John Smith, a native West Virginian who was wounded in action in Shiloh, Virginia during the Civil War, and re-enlisted for another year following his convalescence.

Donald Smith has four siblings, Bill, Ed, Fred and Ann, who also attended schools in West Virginia. Donald enjoyed regular sports and his favorite was track.

When Donald was 17 years old, his mother signed his enlistment papers, and Donald began a naval career that spanned over 30 years. He entered the Navy in July 1959 and was sent to Great Lakes, Illinois for basic and advanced training. He continued his training in September 1959 at the Naval Training Center, where he began training as a Gunners Mate working in the armory on small arms maintenance and repairs. In February of 1961 he was transferred to the USS Cambria APA 36 until August 1962, the day he turned 21 years old. After a brief stint as a civilian Donald re-enlisted in the Navy in October 1962. He was assigned to the USS Stormes DD 780. During his time on both the USS Cambria and the USS Stormes his units spent a majority of their time in and around Cuba during the Castro uprising.

In 1965 Don was transferred to the USS Brumby DE (FF) 1044 as a new construction ship, commissioning the ship in Charleston, SC. In 1968 Donald was again transferred to Naval Recruit Training Command Great Lakes, IL for a tour of Duty as a Recruit Company Commander. Following this tour at Great Lakes, Donald was transferred to the USS Parsons DDG-19, a forward deployed ship home ported in Yokosuka, Japan. The main purpose of forward deployed ships were quick access to the coastal waters of Vietnam, having spent numerous cruises off the coast, his ship was there for the conclusion of hostile actions. Donald then transferred to the USS Francis Hammond FF-1067 for the remainder of his tour in Japan.

Returning to Great lakes in 1977, Donald completed another shore duty assignment at Service School Command serving as an instructor. In September 1980 Donald returned to sea aboard the USS Tattnall, serving as the senior enlisted advisor. In October 1982, Donald was commissioned a Chief Warrant Officer and was assigned to the USS Coral Sea CV-43 until 1985.

Donald concluded his 30 plus years of Naval service as a CWO4, with a tour at the Naval Amphibious Base in Little Creek, Virginia retiring in February 1990.

Donald received several ribbons and medals for his service, which include the Navy Commendation Medal (4), Navy Achievement (2), Combat Action, Good Conduct (4), AFEM, Vietnam Service and Campaign medals to name a few.

After his naval service Donald held several jobs until he moved to Florida in 1997, with his wife Frances who was with him on his journey of Naval Service. They have four children (Diane, Donna, Frank, and Steven, eight grandchildren and 2 great grandchildren.

Donald is very active in Veterans affairs in Osceola County, member of the VFW, American Legion, Fleet Reserve, Navy League, Military Officers Association, and is the Chairman of the Museum of Military History located in Kissimmee.

VIETNAM WAR—A CIVIL WAR—(North Vietnam against South Vietnam)

The Vietnam War—I am not going to pretend to know what caused the United States to ever get involved in that war in the first place. A country divided doesn't happen overnight, at first you don't see it, and suddenly it had happened.

Once again I was fortunate to be able to interview several of the Veterans that served during and in the Vietnam War. And I am happy to learn that some of the scars from that war are starting to heal.

Since the dedication of the "Wall" (National Vietnam Veterans Memorial) was dedicated there has begun an essential healing process for many Vietnam Veterans to forgive and forget the unpleasantness that welcomed them during their homecoming from the war.

Surely they know that not all Americans felt bitter or were bitter about that time in our history. And that the majority of Americans during the war and still today are proud of the men and women that fought during the Vietnam War, just as much as they are proud of the men and women that fought any of the other wars that the United States was involved in.

On the other hand we can understand your bitterness, hopefully your scars will heal in time, and you will forgive those that put them there in the first place. And know that in our hearts that we feel your suffering.

WOMEN that served during VIETNAM—On 11 November 1993, the Vietnam Women's Memorial was dedicated honoring women in military service during the Vietnam War. It was the first Memorial ever honoring female military Veterans. It is located on the grounds of the Vietnam Veterans Memorial, the "Wall", in Washington, DC. Of the 265,000 Women that served during the twelve years of the Vietnam War, none were drafted.

Easton, John D. (Doug)	United States Navy
Chief Electricians Mate	Korea, Vietnam

Doug was born 16 January 1934 in Quincy, Massachusetts and grew up in Dorchester, Massachusetts. He graduated from Dorchester High School. Doug has two younger sisters, Anne and Judith.

Doug enlisted in the United States Navy in August 1953, at the age of 19, and spent twenty-six years serving his country. After boot camp and his first tour, he was discharged and transferred to the US Naval Reserves until he was recalled to active duty in October 1961 during the Berlin crisis. That was when he decided to make the Navy his life's career.

Doug's duty stations were Naval Training Command, Bainbridge, Maryland (Boot Camp); EM "A" School, Service Schools Command, Great Lakes, Illinois; USS Atka (AGB-3); USS Miller (DD 585); USS Hazelwood (DD 531); USS Compton (DD 705); Service Craft, Naval Shipyard, Portsmouth, New Hampshire; EM "B" School, Service

Command, Great Lakes, Illinois; USS Fairfax County (LST 1193); USS LY Spear (AS-36) And Supervisor of Shipbuilding and Repair (SUPSHIP) Boston, Massachusetts.

During his naval career, Doug spent eighteen years at sea including two Operation Deep Freeze cruises to the Antarctic onboard the USS Atka (AGB-3) and has visited many ports around the world. It shows, anytime his wife asks if they can take a trip to anywhere overseas the answer he gives is "Why, I've already been there?"

Doug retired from the US Navy 19 November 1979. His retirement ceremony was conducted on board the USS Constitution at the Charlestown Navy yard in Charlestown, Massachusetts.

Doug was awarded the National Defense Medal, Good Conduct Medal (5 Awards) and the Antarctic Service Medal during his career.

Doug has no regrets about his chosen career path of serving in the military.

After his retirement from the US Navy, Doug was not able to enjoy a second career with one company because his present wife was still on active duty with the US Navy. Instead he used his talents working for several defense contractors all over the country, such as, CDI Marine Corporation in Norwell, Massachusetts and PRC Gorlnick/Envisions, Inc, San Diego, California as a Senior Marine Electrical Designer, ROH, Crystal City, Virginia as a Marine Technical Writer, Rosenblatt & Sons, San Diego, California, Senior Marine Electrical Designer, a short tour working onboard the USS John F Kennedy at the Philadelphia Shipyard, Atlantic Ordnance, Norfolk, Virginia, and again at CDI Marine Corporation in Newport News and Portsmouth, Virginia as a Senior Electrical Designer.

He retired from CDI Marine Corporation July 2002 to travel with his wife, Gail, cross-country in their motor home. They spent two wonderful years on the road before settling in the State of Florida in 2004. Even after coming to Florida, they spent the next several years living in the motor home and periodically travelling to the west coast—what a life!

 Doug is married to Gail (Loveday) Easton, a retired US Navy veteran also mentioned in this book. He has four children (two boys and two girls) and one stepdaughter from a previous marriage and three stepdaughters from his present marriage.

The Easton's main activity is roller skating. He started as a youngster of 8 or 9 going to the rink with his sister, Anne, because that is where all the girls were. The girls were always looking for a boy to skate the dances with. It made no difference if you knew the dance or not, the girls would teach you. Eventually he started taking lessons, got a partner and started competing. With his present wife, they had a moderately successful skating career. They have competed out of four different regions and won or placed in all their respective regional championships to qualify to skate the US National Roller Skating Championships.

They also have progressed through the elimination round to skate the finals in the Masters Dance Division at the US National Roller Skating Championships. Now they skate for fun and friendships. It is always good to get up a conversation with one of your old competitors. The stories seem to change as the years go by, but they have fun. Between the military and roller skating they have shared a long and active life.

Doug is a member of USA Roller Sports (USARS) as a "B" Commissioned Artistic Roller Skating Judge, Roller Skating International (RSA) as a Level "4" Achievement Test Judge, the Florida Chief Petty Officer Association (FLCPOA) and the American Legion, Post 65, Dorchester, Massachusetts.

Easton, Gail Marie United States Navy
Chief Yeoman Vietnam, Desert Storm
08/03/1974-01/31/1997 Thirteen Duty Stations

For a small frame lady, this Chief Yeoman had a whole lot of activity going on after she joined the United States Naval Reserve; she spent twenty-three years serving her country.

Gail Marie (Loveday) Easton was born on 11 December 1941 in Brockton, Massachusetts, Gail grew up with her nine siblings, six girls and four boys, and she was the third in line. Their mother was a Registered Nurse and their father owned his own radio, appliance and television business. Gail said from the time he was a teenager her father knew what he liked doing and was good at it; he built and sold his first radio when he was sixteen.

While growing up Gail attended Howard Elementary School, North Junior High School and Brockton High School. It didn't end there for Gail, she continued her education attending Quincy Junior College and Northeastern University in Massachusetts and St Leo College/St Leo University (military campus, South Hampton Roads, Norfolk/Virginia Beach, Virginia) where she graduated with an Associates of Arts in Liberal Arts, Bachelors of Science in Computer Information Systems and a Bachelors of Arts in Business Administration. Gail also attended Coleman College in La Mesa, California where she graduated with an Associates of Science in Computer Information Science.

On 3 August 1974, at the age of 32, Gail joined the US Naval Reserves under the Advanced Pay Grade Program as a drilling reservist and six months later was recalled to active duty at Naval Air Station South Weymouth, Massachusetts as a TAR (Training and Administration of Reserves).

Gail Loveday, her maiden name; was not the first or the last of the ten sisters and brothers to join the military. The second in line, brother, Edward Loveday, served in the US Navy, sister, Marie, the fifth born, served in the US Naval Reserves, one set of twins (there are two sets); seventh & eighth born; Jack served in the US Navy and twin brother, Charlie did a tour with the US Air Force. Gail's sister, Diane (also a twin) and the tenth born, served nine years in the US Air Force as a Medic. Gail mentioned she has several cousins that also served in the US military. She believes the Loveday clan had all the services covered!

The Loveday children that served in the military had a good mentor, their grandfather Loveday was retired from the US Marine Corps and served actively in the Spanish American War and World War I. Later in this story you will learn about Gail's own offspring that also served in the military.

During her military career, Gail certainly can feel a great sense of accomplishment; she has served with honor at thirteen military duty stations. Following is a listing of those stations; as a drilling reservist: NAVSHOREACT 101, Naval Reserve Station, Brockton, MA and NARDIV1, Naval Air Station (NAS) South Weymouth, MA; active duty: Naval Air Station South Weymouth, MA, Personnel Support Detachment (the first PSD in the country), NAS South Weymouth, MA, Naval Air Reserve Unit (NARU), NAS Norfolk, VA, Naval & Marine Corps Reserve Center (NMCRC), Fields Point, Providence, RI, Naval Reserve Readiness Command Nineteen (NAVRESREDCOM19), San Diego, CA, Fleet Composite Squadron Thirteen, designation changed during her tour to Fleet Fighter Composite Squadron Thirteen (VC/VFC 13), NAS Miramar, San Diego, CA, Naval Air Facility (NAF) Washington, DC, Andrews Air Force Base, Camp Springs, MD, Fleet Logistics Support Squadron Fifty Seven (VR-57), NAS North Island, San Diego, CA, Naval Air Joint Reserve Base (NJRB)Willow Grove, PA and Commander in Chief Atlantic Fleet (CINCLANT), Norfolk, VA.

As Mobilization Officer at two commands and fifteen years as a Navy Instructor, Gail had the tools to ready others for overseas duties; therefore, she was more valuable in that capacity rather than being sent in harm's way. After receiving orders to VR-57, she completed all her overseas screening with the expectation of joining the squadron in Germany where the squadron was deployed performing joint duty with the US Air Force during Desert Storm. The squadron returned to San Diego one week before Gail reported.

One incident Gail will never forget is her ability or non-ability for shooting a pistol. During her first tour on active duty each sailor was authorized thirty rounds each year to qualify for a ribbon. Out of her thirty rounds she hit the target four times! The instructor, being patient wanted to try something else. He gave her his "personal" pistol (a Saturday night special) and loaded it with a .350 Magnum shell. Gail took the pistol, aimed and fired. The backlash was unexpected, needless to say, there is now a hole in the range roof and she figured it safer not to try to qualify ever again.

Highlighting her military achievements Gail said that she has no regrets, that the high points of her march through her Navy career is that of receiving two Navy Achievement Medals; earned at each of her squadrons for taking both of their Administrative Departments from inspection failures to the top Administrative Departments in the Wing. She announced that she did not do it alone, that she had good sailors working for her and they deserve most of the credit. She took a swap to go to VC-13. It was her first tour in Administration. Her friend and shipmate, YN1 Bonnie Tracy, who was the Career Counselor at REDCOM 19 in San Diego, was an Admin wizard. Bonnie gave of herself and came to the squadron nightly afterhours with Gail, helped Gail learn Admin and straighten out the mess. Gail was selected for Chief Petty Officer while at VC-13. YN1 Tracy is the one Gail said that should have been there and the one to make chief.

Along with all that Gail accomplished during her twenty-three year career in the United States Navy, there was also much sorrow with the loss of friends and shipmates. Being a certified Red Cross Water Safety Instructor she was designated to administer the swim qualifications and re-qualifications to all the Navy and Marine Corps pilots and aircrew at NAS South Weymouth.

Gail was very close with the aircrews. She lost several of her friends/shipmates in a boating accident while they were on a training mission to NAS Fallon, Nevada. Gail lost her commander during a S-2 training flight when they lost the generators to both engines over Cape Cod and still another dear friend when piloting his personal plane while off duty.

Gail retired from the United States Navy on 31 January 1997, for her military service she has earned the Navy Achievement Medal (2 awards), Good Conduct medal (5 awards) Armed Forces Reserve medal (Hourglass), Air Force Outstanding Unit Award and National Defense medal.

Gail's military family continued with her children joining the Armed Forces. Her youngest daughter, Joanne, retired after spending twenty years in the US Coast Guard. Joanne's son; Gail's grandson, Ryan did a tour in the US Coast Guard and, Ryan's brother, Jeffrey, is serving with the US Navy. Gail's oldest daughter, Kelly's daughter, Jamie, while serving as a Military Policeman in the US Army in Afghanistan was blown off a humvee by an IED, injured and received a medical discharge. Jamie's brother, Jonathan, is presently serving in the US Army Reserve, attending college, and anticipates receiving his officer commission upon graduation.

Gail after her retirement from the US Navy finished her college education and became a roller skating instructor/coach. She has many regional champions/placements and national placements to her coaching credit.

Gail married her present husband, John Douglas Easton 30 September 1984. Doug is also a Retired Navy Veteran featured in this book.

Highlights of Gail's skating career, she started skating at 9 years old and quit skating when she first married at age 21. She did some competition during that time period, but never placed out of the state championships. Gail returned to skating at the age of 35 at the urging of her children (they wanted to take skating lessons). About a year later she met her now husband, Doug, when he came to the rink with his children.

Doug had just transferred to SUPSHIP, Boston for his "twilight" tour in the Navy and she was only beginning her career in the Navy. They started skating as dance partners in 1978, that partnership was interrupted in 1980 when Gail transferred to NARU, NAS Norfolk, VA. Doug remained in Massachusetts as he had just been hired for an excellent position following his retirement in 1979. They did not skate dance together again until 1986 when Gail was stationed in San Diego, CA. In the interim Gail qualified for nationals several times skating in the Classic Ladies Figure Division. When they commenced skating dances again in 1986 they skated competitively until 1995 when Doug suffered his second heart attack.

During their competitive careers they skated out of four different regions (there are nine regions in the country) and won or placed in each of those regions at their respective regional championships in dance and/or figures which qualified Gail & Doug to skate the US National Championships.

July 1988 was a particularly good month for them. It started well; they placed second in the Masters Dance Division at the Southwest Pacific Regional Championships in Bakersfield, CA. At the end of the championships, Gail skated and passed her Proficiency/Achievement Gold Medal in American Dance. The best of all came when they arrived home from regionals, Gail found out she was selected for Chief Petty Officer. Now that was a great month!

Above is a combined plaque of all of **Gail & Doug Easton's** military awards, they are proud of what they have accomplished in the military and skating together, and so are we.

A few years later, 1990 was a great year for skating; Gail and Doug Easton won the Southeast Regional's in the Masters Dance Division and at the US Nationals in Pensacola, Florida qualified for the finals. That was their best competitive year as the following year Doug suffered his first heart attack a few months before regional's—which they skated and still won.

Gail and Doug moved to Florida in December 2004 after two years on the road in their motor home and after the hurricanes. Gail has three children and five step-children and still roller skates for fun.

Gail is a member of USA Roller Sports (Roller Skating Coach & "B" Commissioned Artistic Competitive Judge), Roller Skating Association International (RSA)(Level "4" Achievement Test Judge), Society of Roller Skating Teachers Association (SRSTA) (Roller Skating Instructor), Florida Chief Petty Officers Association (FLCPOA), Fleet Reserve Association (FRA), American Legion, Post 1, Titusville, FL, and with her hobby of building miniatures, she belongs to the Brevard County Association of Miniaturists (BAM).

Although Gail has had an interesting and full career and life, she still has a few goals that she wishes to accomplish. One is a trip to Ireland where her grandmother and great-grandparents were born and raised and the other to return to Germany where Doug's youngest daughter lives.

Gail loves traveling in their motor home and traveling Space "A".

Johnson, William F.(Bill)   United States Navy
E-7 Chief Petty Officer   Tenn., Calif., New York,
Chief Avionics Technician   Florida, Philippines and
07/1962-01/31/1982   Vietnam

William F. Johnson, (Bill), was born 24 May 1944, in Cleveland, Ohio, and grew up in the town of Willoughby, Ohio (20 mi. east of Cleveland) with his older sister Dawn and younger brother Thomas. Bill said that his father had built the house that they grew up in and he helped his father build it; and that he was eleven years old at the time. Bill's father had a degree in architectural engineering and taught Industrial Arts and Mechanical Drawing at the Junior High School. He told me that his sister Dawn and her family still live in that house today.

One of Bill's fondest memories growing-up was that he arrived home from school one day and sitting in his kitchen was Clown from the Barnum and Bailey Circus; he said that when he stood up the clown was 8'4" tall, he said the clown was a friend of his mother's.

Bill attended and graduated from North High in Eastlake, Ohio (1958-1962). Right out of High School Bill entered the US Navy, he was eighteen years old and did his Basic Training in Great Lakes, Illinois; outside of Chicago.

During his twenty years serving our country Bill spent his first four years going to classes; first at NATTC (Naval Air Technical Training Center) Millington, TN (Avionics Class A School); and graduated June 63, and VS 31 NAS North Island, San Diego, California (1963-1965) Avionics Tech (E-4 to E5, ATTC Millington, TN (Avionics Class B School) and graduated in July 1966.

After much training & learning Bill was stationed at VP 40 NAS (Naval Air Station), North Island, San Diego, CA (1966-67) Avionics Tech deployed to Stangley Field NAS in the Philippines. During this stretch of his career Bill served in Vietnam for two months.

From 1967-1969, Bill served as Avionics Tech (E6) at VS 21 North Island, San Diego, CA.

Bill was a Navy Recruiter from 1969-1972 at NAVCRUITSTA (Naval Recruiting Station) New York. For the next five years, Bill served aboard the USS Independence CV62 (a very large Aircraft Carrier)(1972-1977) as ASCAC Maintenance Supervisor (E7).

Bill's last duty station was in Jacksonville, Florida at VS-30 NAS Cecil Field performing various managerial positions (1977-1982).

On a sunny Saturday morning in San Diego, as Bill wandered the streets, he heard organ music and saw the door to the skating rink was open so he stopped in to investigate.

What he saw turned out to be club practice. One of the club members discovered him leaning on the railing and invited him in. It wasn't long before he was introduced to Elmer Reingeisen, (his first skating coach) and Cindy (his first dance partner). This was the beginning of what turned out to be a life long affair with roller dance skating.

Bill started taking skating lessons and within a year of skating Bill was in competition at Regional's in Bakersfield, California in 1984. He continued skating throughout his Navy career, he met his first and second wife skating, and he still skates today and usually can be found at Reflections Skating Rink in Kissimmee, Florida with his wife Irene, also a professional skater.

US Navy Veteran William F. Johnson (Bill) retired from the Navy on 31 January 1982. For his military service he earned 5 Good Conduct Medals, the Distinguished Service Medal among other medals and ribbons.

Bill's brother Thomas served also in the U.S. Navy for ten years, and was stationed on the USS Enterprise; he had gotten sick because of the asbestos he was exposed to on the ship, and Thomas ended up with pulmonary ferocious, sadly he passed away at age sixty-six years.

After his Military career Bill went to work at the Allen Bradley Company as a Technical Instructor from 1982 till 2009. He also taught classes such as Programmable Logic Controllers, Graphic Interfaces, Networks and Safety Controllers.

Some of Bill activities and interest are FRA (Fleet Reserve Assn.), American Legion Member, Professional Roller Skating and Golf. He moved to Florida Halloween of 2005, he is the father of two children; a daughter named Elizabeth and a son Donald, and has four grandchildren, all girls. No regrets.

Buck, Paul K.	United States Army
Artillery—Cook	Vietnam War
05/19/1965-1967	Ft. Carson, CO

Paul was born two days after President Franklin D. Roosevelt died (12 April 1945), he was born on 14 April; surely this event took away the attention of this new born baby to Mr. and Mrs. Buck. Paul was born on that day in a rural neighborhood in Indianapolis, Indiana; he also grew up and went to school along with his one sister and three brothers in Indianapolis.

Paul's brother Brad, the youngest, served in the U.S. military and now lives with Paul in Florida, during Brad's military service he was stationed in Germany.

Their brother Luke also served in the United States military, and was an ambitious Artist with the U.S. Army. Paul's third brother's name was Tom and their sister's name is Sally; his sister recently turned eighty-eight-years-old, she is the oldest and amazingly still lives in the area they grew up in, Indianapolis, Indiana.

Some of Paul's fondest memories are those while growing up and attending school in Indianapolis, Paul said that his most favorite teacher was Mr. Barnett, the teacher that took the opportunity and time to tech Paul the art of writing poetry. Paul has written many inspirational poems; some of which are included in this book.

Going back to his childhood, Paul told me about an incident he remembered when he was ten years old. He said that his parents put him into a hospital, because they were told by several doctors that he had cancer. It was a devastating time for the whole family, and after spending about four months in the hospital and going through several test and procedures, Paul's parents were thankful to learn that that their son Paul did not have cancer after all.

After he graduated from high school, Paul held a few different positions, until he turned twenty years old and was called-up by the U.S. draft. Our Uncle Sam wanted him to come and join the troops that were fighting the North Vietnamese. At that time the military was recruiting everyone they could get; because at that time the Vietnam War was at its peak.

On 5 October 1965 Paul was mustered into the Army, first he was sent to Fort Knox for basic training, and then sent to Fort Still, Oklahoma for extended training.

He was assigned to "C" Battery, 16th Artillery. As soon as he finished advance training, Paul received his orders for Vietnam.

Paul told me that just before the Thanksgiving Holiday, the 16th Artillery group had a horrible accident that occurred causing the death of four-soldiers. One of the wounded died in the arms of Paul Buck, an incident that still hurts him to talk about; the soldier's name was Leon Fox. Another soldier that died in the accident was cut in half, his name was Thurman Adair, and the fact that Adair only had four months more to serve before being discharged was heartfelt throughout "C" Company.

While serving in Vietnam Paul was smack in the middle of the epic struggle from attacks attempted against their positions.

During the Christmas Holiday, several days of cease fire were initiated, but on 27 December 1966 an attack by the NVA occurred.

From the archives history the incident went like this:

On 26th December, B Company received orders through a radio call from the acting Battalion 53 Operations Officer to occupy blocking positions in a valley about 3-4 kilometers just to the south of "LZ Bird" at the base of Crow's Foot Mountains during a so-called Christmas truce.

During that evening they were surprised as to why a series of small but persistent probing NVA attacks were attempted against their positions.

In the early morning hours of 27 December, all hell broke lose; when heavy artillery, rockets, and small arms fire just to the North, in what they later found out was a major attack by the elements of the 22nd NVA Regiment against "LZ Bird", where two artillery batteries were located.

"LZ Bird" was also being defended by troops of "C" Company that was still recuperating from the 506 Valley incidents just ten days or so earlier.

Paul Buck was part of "C" Company that serviced the artillery during that attack. Paul quickly adapted to the tropical climate and the constant threat of attack that pervaded all areas of Vietnam.

After finishing his tour of duty, Paul was honorably discharged in 1976, following his discharge from the US Military Paul obtained employment with Trans World Airlines (TWA), later American Airlines. Paul retired

after thirty-eight years with the same company.

Paul Buck was married to Linda Toney; they were married thirty-nine years before she died in 2009. Together they had two sons, Jason, living in Charlotte, NC and Adam living in Ohio. Paul also has three granddaughters and one grandson.

He is a member of the VFW and the American Legion in Osceola County and on the Board of Directors at the Museum of Military History, in Kissimmee, Florida.

Paul also is often a guest speaker at the local schools where he lives, he talks about his experiences while serving during the Vietnam War; and he often receives letters from the students and teachers thanking him for his interest and support in helping them learn our military history.

Paul said he has no regrets and the high lite of his lifetime is when he met his wife Linda Toney. The following poem is one that Paul wrote.

GUILT

I have to wonder sometimes
If I'm really worth the price
What have I done or what can I do
That could be worth a human life

I served long ago in Vietnam
With men as brave as any
And I understand that brave men die
But Lord must there be so many

It's hard to comprehend
No matter how I try
Is it just a crapshoot
Who will live or die

Or were we chosen
We who survive

Is there some reason
Why we are still alive

This feeling of guilt I'll always have
Simply for being alive
When so many other brave young men
Were somehow unable to survive

By, Paul Buck

Krol, Edmund P. CM2	U.S. Navy Coast Guard (Seabee)
NMCB—14 D 0414	Cleveland Harbor, New Orleans
01/1966-09/1971-R-72	Mackinaw Ice Breaker

Edmund Krol was no stranger to the water, he was born 29 July 1942, in Cleveland, Ohio, and he attended parochial grade school and Benedictine High, graduating in 1960.

While traveling to school and various sporting events at the Cleveland lakefront stadium, he would watch the different freighters, tugs, and the Coast Guard boats stationed at Whiskey Island, performing many duties around the harbor.

At age twenty-three years his fascination with the water still existed causing him to enlist in the United States Coast Guard Reserves, and was sent to boot camp at Cape May, New Jersey.

From there he went to Great Lakes training in diesel engines, and then on to the Ice Breaker Mackinaw with the Coast Guard's Ice Breaker, serving all the Great Lakes.

Ed's Reserve duty training stations included firefighting and damage control while serving in Groton, CT. Also Instructor Training at Yorktown, VA, Relief Engineman, and engine overhaul at Cleveland Harbor, as well as serving as a Engineman 2nd class aboard the Coast Guard Cutter-Buoy Tender at Ojibowa Base, Buffalo, New York.

After completing his six year enlistment and having moved to Florida fulltime, Ed applied some of his acquired skills in the heavy diesel, mining equipment, used in Central Florida. It was during this time through the workings of a Seabee friend he was introduced and recommended to enlist in the Navy Seabee Reserves.

After completing a physical and training exam with an update in weaponry, at Camp Blanding, Florida he was A.P.G. to his E. 5 discharge rate. Ed was assigned to Reserve Unit NCB-14 out of Jacksonville.

Ed served two years with two reenlistments when a motorcycle wreck number two cut his military career short.

After his discharge and hard year of healing he worked as a Diesel Instructor for Ridge Votec, Polk County Schools in Florida.

Ed continues to live in Polk Count, Florida with his wife Meredith of twenty years and is looking forward in his retirement years to visit his old ship the Mighty Mac.

ICE BREAKER—MACKINAW (Mighty Mac)

The Icebreaker Mackinaw (Mackinaw City, Michigan) is a 290 foot (88m) Vessel designed for ice breaking duties on the Great Lakes. The Mackinaw was home-ported in Cheboygan, Michigan during her active service. This magnificent piece of machinery can proceed through fresh water ice up to 20 inches thick and break ice up to three feet thick, through ramming. These vessels are equipped with a system to lubricate their progress through the ice, by bubbling air through the hull.

The cutter was decommissioned and replaced with a smaller multipurpose cutter (the USCGC Mackinaw (WLBB-30), which was commissioned in Cheboygan the same day. The old Mackinaw moved under its own power on 1 June 2006 from the Port of its decommissioning to a permanent berth (at the SS Chief Wawatam dock) at the ships namesake port, Mackinaw City, Michigan, where she now serves as the Ice Breaker Maritime Museum.

The following story was told by a Navy Seabee Veteran while serving in Vietnam; you will read about him following the story.

BOOM/BOOM in I CORP

1966—The story starts in a place called PhuBai, Republic of Viet Nam in the summer of 1966. My Seabee outfit named Naval Mobile Construction Battalion Seven was attached to the 3rd Marine Division. Our camp of 800+ men was located in a Buddhist cemetery about sixty miles south of North Vietnam.

As a twenty year-old E-4, I was ordered to engineer, supervise the construction, and protect a heavy—duty fifty foot span-bridge over a creek, in an area primarily controlled by the Viet Cong and at least 10 miles from the nearest Americans. According to protocol, I knew a Chief or above should be in charge of this project; not a 3rd Class Petty Officer A crazy Marine colonel wanted to run his tanks over it. I asked the Col. who was going to protect it after it was finished? He replied; a RVN Army squad. I laughed and told him the ARVN couldn't protect their own mother; then carried out my orders. The bridge was finished two weeks later. It only took the VC one week to blow it up.

1967—On my second tour, I was in Danang East in 1967. As an E-5, I was ordered to engineer and supervise the construction of a major above-ground aviation-gas fuel-tank, as an addition to the Air Force jet fuel farm on a hillside. (For those that don't know, AV gas as we called it is highly explosive and JP-4 jet fuel is like diesel fuel and under normal conditions will not explode). I asked my superior officer to let me bury it fifteen feet underground with heavy creosoted timbers cross hatched on top of the tank to protect it from enemy rocket and mortar fire. It was just a little more work. He said no do as ordered.

This time, remembering my bridge, I appealed my idea all the way up the chain of command to our battalion Commanding Officer. He said, do as ordered. I went back to my desk and stewed about it some more. Then I did something I should not have according to military protocol. I called up the naive Air Force Colonel base commander that ordered it and explained my position. As soon as he found out I was a lowly enlisted man, he cussed me up one side and down the other and slammed the phone down. I asked myself who I contact next: LBJ? I was out of options, I did as ordered. The AF Colonel called our CO and chewed him out about my phone call. I was called to the C.O.'s office and told by the CO that I needed some leadership training. I would be immediately transferred from engineering and be placed in charge of the mess cooks at the chow hall. Two weeks later the aviation fuel tank was finished.

Three weeks afterward, in June of 1967 there was a major daytime rocket attack around the fuel farm. I was standing with about six other Seabees on our west perimeter watching the attack from five miles away. One rocket made a direct hit on my above ground tank, followed by a 5,000 foot fire ball. It looked just like a nuclear explosion; mushroom cloud and all. A few seconds later the shock wave hit us and blew all of us off our feet (from 5 miles away). Later, I went over to the fuel farm. Everything was leveled and burned and buildings were ashen up to 1.5 miles out. I do not know how many casualties there were, but it had to be many. I'm sure the AF Col. blamed it on the VC and said nothing about my recommendation; he refused.

No planes operated out of Danang for two weeks. Then, the Air Force temporary pumped fuel to the planes directly from the tankers in the harbor via rubber pipeline.

No one said anything to me about the fuel farm; I was still in charge of the mess cooks.

By Raymond Cochran (Seabee)

NMCB-7 (attached to the 3rd Marine Division Vietnam 1966-67)

Cochran, Raymond	U. S. Navy (Seabees)
MNCB	Vietnam War
01/1966-1968	PhuBai, RVN and Danang, RVN

Ray Cochran was born on 5 November 1944, while World War Two was still going on. He grew up and attended schools along with his brother, in Boston, Massachusetts. Ray's father served in the military before and during World War Two and Korea, he was a Corpsman in the Navy and before retiring was awarded the rank of Warrant Officer. Ray's brother Eric also served in the U.S. Navy and advanced to officers status before retiring after twenty-three years.

When Ray turned seventeen years old he enlisted in the Navy Seabee Reserves. After finishing his written and physical exam, he was sworn in and shipped to Great Lakes, Illinois for his basic training. Ray also trained at the Marine Base, Camp Lejeune, NC. After finishing all his military training he was assigned to MNCB-7 (Mobil Navy Construction Battalion-7).

Ray's first duty station when he arrived in Vietnam was Camp Campbell. He was also at Phu Bai, 65 miles South of North Vietnam. Ray said an incident that took place while he was doing Jeep Patrol out of the Phu Bai area; they had just left the pavement and proceeded down the dirt roads that turned into rutted paths. About an hour out and

15 miles from the nearest Americans, they were approaching a village; it was then when he saw a gook standing on the edge of the jungle on the other side of the rice paddy 59 yards away, staring intently at their patrol. He was wearing black pajamas, a straw hat and carrying a M1 carbine. He looked like a stereotype "VC" to Ray. Ray asked permission to plug him, (he quoted the rule which was don't fire, unless fired on first). The LT. replied, "Hold your fire; he is probably a South Vietnamese Militia"

They rolled through the village at maximum safe speed of 5 mph; the rutty trail was that bad! After another mile they jostled into a sand dune area; Ray knew they were near the coast, the dunes were 10 to 20 feet tall, and they could travel no more than 5 mph.

About ten minutes into the dunes, the LT. announced that he was getting hungry and ordered them to turn around and head back to camp for lunch. They did a five point turn between the dunes, because there was so little maneuvering room and pushed back to the paved road.

The next afternoon, the Marine grunt battalion camped next door and asked their battalion if they had any jeeps in that coastal area the day before? They informed him that they had a jeep patrol in the area. It was then that the Marine stated that they had a foot patrol in the same area this morning and had discovered a VC ambush site about 50 yards further from where they had turned around. The Marine said; the VC had a platoon ready for them on both sides of the dunes with three machine guns and that it was a perfect cross fire for the VC.

Ray's group soon realized that they were lucky, that the gook with the M1 was a lookout for the ambush; and they would have been annihilated. The Marines asked us why we turned around, we told them about the LT's hunger pains and the group said thank God for that; Ray said it was only one of many of his close calls.

After serving four years with the Navy Seabee Reserves, Ray was discharged in the war zone; "he has expressed to me that he hasn't heard of anyone else being discharged in the war zone". And it was complicated for him because he needed transportation back to the United States.

For his military service Ray Cochran earned; The Navy Unit Commendation Medal, U.S. Naval Reserve Commendation Medal, National Defense Medal, U.S.N. Expert Riflemen Medal, the Vietnam Service Medal 2/stars, Vietnam Campaign Medal, Republic of Vietnam Gallantry Cross, Republic of Vietnam Citation, among other ribbons and awards.

Ray now lives in Lakeland, Florida with his lovely wife Mary; he is active with several of the Vietnam Veterans groups in the area and served as Commander for the Navy Seabees of America, Island X-2 in Lakeland, Florida.

> **Riley, Richard II (Rick)** U. S. Navy (Seabees)
> Senior Chief E8 (Equip. Opt.) Vietnam Era
> 09/13/1967-04/01/1970 Great Lakes, IL, Davisville,
> RI, Port Hueneme, CA

Rick Riley was born on 6 November 1947, two years after the end of World War Two; in a town called Bremerton, Washington. Rick was born while his father was still serving in the United States Navy; his father was being trained in Annapolis when World War Two broke-out and after graduating in December 1941 from Annapolis Rick's father went from there to the North Atlantic on a Destroyer Escort chasing German subs.

Like most children of military career families; Rick grew up in several towns and states; he grew up in Boston, MA, Washington, DC, Bay City, MI, Des Moines, IA, Port Hueneme, Ca, Davisville, RI, Waukee, IA, Manchester, MI, Urbandale, IA and Honolulu, HI.

Rick was not alone while growing up, he had several sibling, Jim, Kate, Molly, Mark, Margaret, and Meg. His brother Jim was a Career Army Officer; he flew helicopters and was stationed in Vietnam as well. Rick's brother Mark was in the fleet Navy for one enlistment, he was on an aircraft carrier in the Mediterranean.

While growing and learning Rick attended the following schools; Teddy Roosevelt High School, Des Moines, IA, Creighton U, Omaha, NE, Des Moines Area Comm. College, Sienna Heights College, and Adrian, MI.

On 13 September 1967 Rick joined the United States Military, he chose the Navy, after his written and physical examinations, Rick was sworn into the Navy Seabee's, he was nineteen years old at the time at that time the war in Vietnam was raging.

Rick was assigned to take his basic training at Great Lakes, Illinois, a base he was familiar with, since while growing up his father was stationed there. He moved on after basic to camps in Port Hueneme, California and Davisville, Rhode Island.

After finishing all his training Rick was assigned to the NMCB-1, NMCB 25, NMCB 15, 2nd NCR, Fleet Hospital 23, and NMCB 26. Rick's military occupational training title was that of Equipment Operator, and the weapons that Rick learned to use and take care of while he served in the military were; M-14, 3.5 Rocket Launcher, 81MM Mortar, M-16, 45 Caliber Auto, M-60 Machine Gun, and Light Anti-tank Weapon (LAW).

Qualifying as an Equipment Operator Rick's first assignment was to report to NMCB 1, in Davisville, RI, 1968. He said the troops were just coming back from a deployment in Vietnam. His wife "Pam" went with him and they found an apartment off base. Most everyone coming back went on leave. He said he would go to the base and muster each morning then turn around and go home. After being there about a week a big Nor'easter snow storm dumped about 44" of snow in a couple of days.

His wife had found a job in an insurance agency at a car dealer. She called him and asked if he wanted a job shoveling snow, so he went down to the dealership. Arriving at the dealership he noticed a dump truck and front end loader parked there. Nobody knew how to run them. He had just completed EO "A" school and knew how to run both. Instead of shoveling, Rick would load the dump truck go dump it and load it again with the front end loader. When he finished clearing the snow the parts manager asked him if he'd like a job. Rick told him he was in the Navy but would work when he could, the parts manager agreed to that.

About this time the troops began coming back from leave and getting ready to go to schools for more training. Rick wasn't eligible because he just finished A school. He'd muster each morning leave and go to the dealership and work in the parts dept. After about a month his platoon Chief asked what he was doing during the day. He wanted to make sure he wasn't lying around the barracks. Rick was up front with him and told him he wasn't living in the barracks, but off base with his wife. That he had a part time job at a car dealer. The platoon Chief said he'd have to put him on the watch bill and keep doing what he was doing.

Great news! The first week of May the CO said they would be deploying in June. Rick put in for a ten day leave to take his wife home over Memorial Day. When Rick returned he moved into the barracks, they deployed mid month.

They flew into DaNang on a charter from the states. Then boarded a 130 and flew to Hue where he worked in a concrete-ready-mix plant. They paved a lot of highway, poured helo pads for the Marines, made sidewalks and a variety of other things. Finally they closed their camp in Hue and split up into detachments. Rick went to Camp Eagle, the home of the 101st Army Airborne. They had their own compound inside their camp; they ran an asphalt paving plant. They again began paving everything from roads to sidewalks. From there Rick went on a detail to Quang Tri to close a Seabee base down, in November of 1969. The first of the year they closed the asphalt plant down and rejoined the main body in DaNang. Rick came back from his deployment in late March 1970, his two year active duty was up in September, and he was released from active duty on 1 April 1970.

Richard Riley remained in the Reserve program; and stayed in the reserve program until December 2006, after spending 39 years, 2 months, and 23 days; Rick retired as a Senior Chief. For his military service Rick earned and received the National Defense Medal, Vietnam Service Medal, RVN Campaign Medal, the Navy Achievement-2 Medal, the Navy Marine Corp Meritorious Unit Campaign Medal and the Navy E-2 Medal along with several ribbons and other awards. Rick said while he served in Vietnam on Christmas Day 1969, they loaded up a deuce and a half and headed out to the Bob Hope show. He said it was a great show in front of thousands of servicemen.

After his discharge from the military Rick worked in sales and marketing for over thirty years. And his family now has a company that manufactures a line of multipurpose rakes. They started the company in 2001 with prototyping and making the mold for the heads. They went into production early 2002. They received a patent in 2003 and have continued to grow each year into more and more markets; such as tree care, landscaping, golf courses and catalogs as well as retail stores. They have a patented, proprietary product that's made in the United States of America.

Rick is retired and now lives in Waukee, Iowa with his wife Pamela (Pam), they have been married for 45 years and have four sons, Pat, Rusty, Matt and Josh. He is a member of the Blue Lodge, Scottish Rite, Shrine, Life Member of NERA, been a member of VFW, American Legion, Elks, and Moose.

Rick mentioned that the only regret he has is not being able to spend more time with his children while they were growing up. And that the high points are that his family and his thirty-nine years in the Seabees and all the great people he got to work with.

Gerry L. Shatzer U.S. Air Force
Security Police K-9 Lackland Air Force Base
10/1970-12/1971

Born in Chambersburg, Pennsylvania on 19 December 1951, Gerry grew up with his two brothers and two sisters. He attended Cash Schools and after his eighteenth birthday signed up for the United States military service.

Gerry chose the U.S. Air Force and completed his basic training at Lackland Air Force Base where he remained serving his country as a Security Police, in the K-9 Units.

Working as an air Force K-9 Dog handler involves working together with your assigned dog to train and learn how to perform the detection mission. On a single day as many as 108 different dogs may be working and training, with their handlers at the Air Force Base. Dogs are exposed to training regimes that teach both the dog and the handler how to deal with different types of situations. There are two different types of Dog handler missions.

The handlers work with their canines to train and detect explosives, or find drugs in a number of different situations. There are over 1300 working Dog handler teams worldwide, and working dogs from the other branches of the service. The 341st Squadron is responsible for training Dog Handler Teams, and it is located at Lackland Air force Base in San Antonio, Texas.

After being discharged from the military Gerry obtained a position as a Corrections Officer. His resident is in Camp Hill, Pennsylvania. Gerry is an advent roller skater and enjoys tinkering with old cars.

Carmean, Richard Scott, CMDCM (SW/AW/ NAC)
United States Navy
Chief of Naval Operations Directed
Command Master Chief
Naval Air Crewman, Surface Warfare Spec., Air Warfare Spec.,
Federal German Navy Electronic Warfare Air Crewman, Master Training Specialist

CMDCM, R.S. Carmean is a native of Portland, OR; Scott graduated from Benson High School, and subsequently enlisted in the U.S. Navy in 1973.

After completion of Naval Recruit Training at RTC Orlando, FL, Master Chief Carmean received training in the Advanced Electronics Field and designation as an Aviation Electronics (Avionics) Technician at Naval Air Technical Training Center Millington TN. He subsequently served as a technician on the A-6 Intruder attack aircraft, maintaining all aircraft communications, navigation, electronic warning and radar jamming equipment.

From 1974 to 1976, Master Chief Carmean was forward deployed and stationed onboard US Midway (CVA 41) with Attack Squadron (VA) 115 home ported in Yokosuka, Japan. During this tour, in April 1975, He participated in Operation Frequent Wind, the evacuation of Saigon during the fall of the South Vietnamese government. In December of 1976, CMDCM Carmean transferred to VA-165, where he served as an avionics technician and flight deck troubleshooter during the Boomer's nine month long 1977 Western Pacific deployment aboard USS Constellation (CV 64).

Reenlisting for orders to the Navy's enlisted air crewmen program, CMDCM Carmean completed the H-46 Sea Knight fleet replacement maintenance personnel training syllabus with Helicopter Combat Support Squadron (HC) 3 at Naval Air Station (NAS) North Island, CA. Upon completion of training, CMDCM Carmean was assigned to the Search and Rescue team at Operations Department of NAS Cubi Point in the Philippines.

In 1979, CMDCM Carmean converted to the Aviation Anti-Submarine Squadron (VS) 41 at NAS North for Fleet Replacement Air-crewman/ airborne sensor operator training in the S-3 Viking ASW aircraft. Upon completion of training and position qualification in the S-3, he was assigned to the Gamblers of VS-28 at NAS Cecil Field, Florida. The Gamblers completed deployments to the Mediterranean Sea and the Indian Ocean aboard USS Independence (CV 62) while participating in combat operations in Lebanon. During this tour he qualified for and was designated a Naval Air-crewman and Aviation Warfare Specialist.

After completion of his sea duty tour with the Gamblers, Master Chief Carmean was selected for Instructor Duty. He completed instructor training at Naval Air Technical Training Center (NATTC), Millington, TN and was subsequently assigned to the ASW Operator class "A" school. There he taught Nuclear and Conventional, United States' and Warsaw Pact country's, submarine engineering and propulsion systems. During this rewarding tour, CMDCM Carmean was certified and designated as an instructor, as an instructor evaluator, and as a U.S. Navy, Master Training Specialist. In September of 1985, while serving at NATTC Millington, CMDCM Carmean was initiated and promoted to Chief Petty Officer.

As recognition for outstanding service at NATTC Millington, CMDCM Carmean was selected for duty as an advisor to the Federal German Navy's Third Air Wing (ASW) and participation in the U.S. Navy's Personnel Exchange Program (PEP). Prior to execution of these orders, he was first assigned to the Defense Language Institute in Monterey, CA for nine months of intensive training in the German Language. In October of 1986, he transferred to Marinefliegergeschwader Drei, "Graf Zeppelin" (Third German Naval Air Wing "Graf Zeppelin") in Nordholz, West Germany.

The German Air Wing Commander assigned him to the Second Submarine Hunting Squadron (U-boot Jagi Staffel) of the Ai Wing. There he served as the squadron Operations Department Leading Chief Petty Officer (LCPO), and as a member of Combat Aircrew Six as the sensor station coordinator, and as the squadron's assistant aircrew training officer. While with the "Bundesmarine" (Federal German Navy), he completed numerous deployments to Iceland, Norway, and various other NATO countries in support of NATO Cold War ASW operations. He also served as a U.S. Arms and Equipment purchase motivator, explaining to members of the German Bundesrat and Bundestag (German Senators and Parliamentarians,) how they could better spend their defense dollars (Marks) for ASW and Electronic Warfare sensor system upgrades, thus increasing their combat readiness with regards to NATO ASW operations.

During this tour as an Air-crewman, he flew over 1200 hours in the Dassault-Breguet Atlantique long-range ASW and reconnaissance aircraft. On 9 November 1989, the border separating Western from Eastern Germany was effectively opened with the fall of the Berlin Wall. This ended the forty-year cold war in Europe, and took the edge and fun out of NATO Cold War ASW operations against Warsaw Pact nations. During this tour he was promoted to Senior Chief Petty Officer. After the fall of the Berlin Wall, CMDCM Carmean's tour with the Germans ended in the summer of 1990, and he was honored with selection to the U.S. Navy Senior Enlisted Academy (SEA) at the Naval War College in Newport, R.I.

After completion of the SEA, CMDCM Carmean was ordered to the U.S. Naval Oceanographic Office, at Stennis Space Center, MS, there he assumed the duties of Training Support Department (TSD) LCPO, and Composite Warfare Oceanographic Support Modules (CWOSM) Coordinator. As the TSD LCPO, he was responsible for the quality of instruction, and the men and women who wrote, edited, and produced all oceanographic-training materials, supporting worldwide exportable workshops and organic courses taught at the Fleet ASW Training Centers in Norfolk, VA, and San Diego, CA. As CWOSM coordinator he was responsible for all curriculum materials, and the quality of instruction that provided oceanographic products for every field of Naval Warfare: surface warfare, sub-surface warfare, amphibious warfare, special operations (SpecOps,) and air warfare.

In April 1992, CMDCM Carmean was promoted to Master Chief Anti-Submarine Warfare Operator and then applied for selection into the Command Master Chief program. He was selected for the CMC program in the summer of 1992, and issued orders to the Spruance class destroyer, USS Moosbrugger (DD 980), home ported in Charleston, S.C. In 1993 the "Moose" was chosen to serve as Flagship for Commander, Standing Naval Force Atlantic (STANAVFORLANT). In addition to his Moosebrugger Command Master Chief duties, he additionally served as the Standing Naval Force Atlantic Command Master Chief for Rear Admiral Donald A. Dyer, Commander of STANAVFORLANT 1/93, responsible for the 1500 NATO Sailors assigned to the seven NATO ships of the Force.

In September of 1994, Vice Admiral J. Scott Redd, Commander, U.S. Naval Forces Central Command (NAVCENT), selected CMDCM Carmean to serve as the NAVCENT Force Master Chief at NAVCENT, he was responsible for the 15,000 sailors and Marines assigned to the Central Command Area of Operations (AOP). As the NAVCENT Force Master Chief, he had a seat on the Chief of Naval Operations/ Master Chief Petty Officer of the Navy's Senior Enlisted Leadership Panel, which drafted and implemented Navy wide policies. In July of 1995, at the re-commissioning ceremony of the U.S. Fifth Fleet, onboard USS Abraham Lincoln (CVN 72) CMDCM Carmean was designated the first Fifth Fleet Command Master Chief. During this two year tour of duty, forward deployed to Southwest Asia, units assigned to the NAVCENT/Fifth Fleet team conducted nine major real world operations, involving more than 100,000 Sailors and Marines serving at the "Tip of the Spear" including the UNISOM withdrawal of the NATO troops from Somalia.

In the summer of 1996, CMDCM Carmean was selected as the first Bureau of Naval Personnel assigned Command Master Chief for the Navy Flight

Demonstration Squadron, the "Blue Angels". During the show seasons of 1997, 1998, and 1999 the team performed at over 100 Air show sites, deploying in excess of 750 days, and traveling more than 250,000 miles. CMDCM Carmean was responsible for all Blue Angel enlisted personnel, who maintained the eight F/A-18s and one C-130 aircraft, supported team logistics, and completed all administrative tasks that led to outstanding flight demonstrations around the country during these three show seasons.

In November 1999, CMDCM Carmean transferred to the final duty station of his career. As Command Master Chief at Naval Aviation Schools Command (NASC) in Pensacola, Florida, he was responsible for all enlisted curriculum managers, instructors, and support personnel assigned to the four schoolhouses of NASC. On 1 December 2003, Command Master Chief Carmean retired from United States Navy service after completing more than 30 years of active duty. He has graduated from Pensacola Junior College, City University of Seattle, Washington, and University of West Florida, earning associates 03/1943-03/1946 bachelors, and master's degrees in history and applied history.

Command Master Chief Scott Carmean now lives in Kissimmee, Florida with his wife Julie, they have two sons, Chris and Rick. Rick is a Marine at Cherry Point, NC, the Carmean's also have one granddaughter and one grandson. Scott, as I like calling him is a Life Member of the Veterans of Foreign Wars (VFW), the American Legion (Annual Member), U.S. Military Vets Motorcycle Club, Company of Military Historians, DAV (life), and Association of Public Historians.

You can find/visit Command Master Chief Carmean at the Museum of Military History, Inc., where he serves as Executive Director.

The Gulf War (2 August 1990-28 February 1991), code named Operation Desert Storm (17 January 1991-28 February 1991) was a war waged by a U.N. authorized coalition force from 34 nations led by the United States, against Iraq in response to Iraq's invasion and annexation of Kuwait.

The war is also known under other names, such as the Persian Gulf War, First Gulf War, Gulf War I, or the First Iraq War. Kuwait's Invasion by Iraqi troops that began 2 August 1990 was met with international condemnation, and brought immediate economic sanctions against Iraq by members of the U.N. Security Council. U.S. President George H. W. Bush deployed U.S. forces into Saudi Arabia, and urged other countries to send their own forces to the scene.

When the United Nations intervened in Kuwait in 1990, the 24th Infantry Division, which was part of the Rapid Deployment Force, was one of the first units deployed to Southwest Asia. It arrived in 10 large cargo ships of the US Navy Sealift Command.

In the months that followed, the 24th Division played an important part of Operation Desert Shield by providing heavy firepower with its large number of armored vehicles, including 216 M1A1 Abrams tanks. Elements of the division were still arriving in September, and in the logistical chaos that followed the rapid arrival of U.S. forces in the region, the soldiers of the 24th Division were housed in warehouses, airport hangars, and on the desert sand. The 24th remained in relatively stationary positions in defense of Saudi Arabia until additional American forces arrived for Operation Desert Storm.

Once the attack commenced on 24 February, the 24th Infantry Division formed the east flank of the corps with the 3rd Armored Cavalry Regiment. It blocked the Euphrates River valley to cut off Iraqi forces in Kuwait. The 24th Infantry Division performed exceptionally well in the theater. On 26 February, the 24th Division advanced through the valley and captured Iraqi airfields at Jubbah and Tallil.

Despite some of the fiercest resistance of the war, the 24th Infantry Division destroyed the Iraqi formations and captured the two airfields the next day. The 24th then moved east with VII Corps and engaged several

Iraqi Republican Guard Divisions. After the Iraqi force was defeated, the U.N. mandated that the U.S. withdraw from Iraq, ending the Gulf War.

After returning to the United States in spring 1991, the 24th was reorganized with two brigades. In the fall 1994, Iraq again threatened the Kuwait border, and two brigades from the division returned to southwest Asia.

The next Veteran that you will read about was with the 24th Infantry Division during the Gulf War Invasion.

Grimes, Gary R.　　　　　United States Army
Logistics-24thInf.Div.;
194th Maintenance Battalion　　US, Korea, Saudi Arabia
02/1977-08/2007　　　　　Iraq (Gulf War)

Gary Grimes was born in 1953 in Joliet, Illinois, he attended Chaney Grade School and at age fourteen years old, his family moved to Florida; he also has three brothers. Gary's father served in the United States Army during the Korean War and one of his brothers and his youngest son also served in the U.S. Army.

Gary graduated from the Osceola High School in Florida, and to further his education attended and received degrees from the University of Central Florida, the University of Northern Colorado, and the Naval War College. Gary received his BA in Management before entering military service.

In February 1977 Gary signed up for the US Army and attended Basic Training at Fort Jackson, South Carolina. For the next thirty and one-half years he served in a variety of assignments at company through Corps level at different military installations in and out of country. His M.O. (military occupation) was Logistician; dealing with weapons, ammunition, petroleum, supplies, equipment maintenance and transportation.

Listed are several military stations that Gary was assigned to during his military service: Hunter Army Airfield, Georgia; Fort Benning, Georgia; Aberdeen Proving Grounds, Maryland; Fort Lee, Virginia (twice); Korea (twice); Fort Stewart, Georgia; Saudi Arabia and Iraq (Gulf War); Patrick Air Force Base, Florida; Fort Leavenworth, Kansas; Fort Carson, Colorado; St Petersburg, Florida; STRICOM, Orlando, Florida; Newport Naval Base, Rhode Island.

During his military career Gary was promoted to the rank of Colonel, and was awarded several military medals and ribbons. Gary told me that the high lights of his career were commanding the 194th Maintenance Battalion in Korea and serving with the 24th Infantry Division during the "Gulf War". His only regret is that he was never stationed in Hawaii.

Gary Grimes retired from the U.S. Army in August 2007; he now resides in St. Cloud, Florida with his wife Pat. He has four sons and three grandchildren.

He is 1st Vice Chairman of Museum of Military History, Osceola County, Kissimmee, Florida. He is also the "trumpeter" for the Osceola Veterans Council, Florida and works with disabled Veterans in an equine therapy program.

Females in the Navy (WAVES)—During World War One women worked as nurses for the Navy as early as the American Civil War.

In 1908 the United States Navy Nurse Corps was established. During World War One, in 1916 the Navy was able to induct its first female sailors into the US Naval Reserves. Women served around the continental U.S. and in France, Guam and Hawaii, mostly as Yeomen, they worked as radio operators, electricians, draftsmen, torpedo assemblers and a few other jobs. These women were released after the end of the war.

During the Korean War, women in the Naval Reserve were recalled for the Korean War and during the Vietnam War the nurses served aboard the hospital ships.

In the year 1972 women began to enter warfare and aviation fields, and began receiving promotions (officers). In 1974 the Navy became the first service to graduate a women officer. And in 2010 the Department of the Navy announced a policy allowing women to begin serving aboard Navy submarines.

USS Hunley—The USS Hunley (AS-31) was a Submarine tender of the US Navy launched 28 September 1961 and commissioned 16 June 1962. It was decommissioned from the regular Navy in 1995, and in 1995 transferred to the USS Maritime Commission and in 2007 sold for scrap medal. The next veteran in our book worked aboard the USS Hunley (AS-31) as a Maintenance Technician and non-destructive test inspector.

United States Navy Hull Maintenance Tech
Non-Destructive/Test Inspector
USS Hunley(AS-31)Submarine tender
NSSF New London, CT
Kelly Kern 09/1989-09/1994

The youngest Female Veteran in this book, Mrs. Kelly Kern, was born on 6 August 1971, and grew up attending schools in Eufaula-Tulsa, Oklahoma and Jenks; when Kelly graduated from High School, and two weeks before she was to go away to college, Kelly chose her other dream instead. When she was a young girl growing up, Kelly loved being around the water and fortunately her parents lived around lakes; the dream was to be around a larger part of the water and that is why she chose the United States Navy.

She took herself down to the recruiting office and enlisted in the United States Navy. After completing her paper work and passing her physical

Kelly was sworn in, and after finishing her Basic training in Orlando, Florida, Kelly was sent to Philadelphia for HT-A-training. She chose a male dominate position as her military occupation.

Upon completing her training, Kelly was assigned to the USS Hunley (AS-31) a Submarine tender (repair ship) located in New London, Connecticut. While serving on the Hunley, this little Wave was doing Hull maintenance work; her military occupation title was that of a Maintenance Technician, Kelly also did Non-Destructive Test Inspections.

She said that once while on duty she was sent to the Reactor Compartment to do a reading, this she did for the first time all alone; this was on ultrasonic equipment, a reactor, measuring and taking the levels of water, Kelly had to admit that she was very excited and that is was one of the high lights of her military career.

While going to school in Philadelphia Kelly met her husband Nick, who was also in the U.S. Navy, they were attending school at the same time; he had joined the Navy two years earlier. Kelly married Nick while she was still serving and after five years in the Navy, she decided that it would best for her children if she left the military.

Kelly received an honorable discharge in Portsmouth, Virginia and was awarded the Humanitarian Service Medal, Enlisted Surface Warfare Specialist Medal among other ribbons and awards.

Since her discharge, Kelly and her family have been living in Texas, and have been employed with the Texas Department of Public Safety, working as an Investigator for Compliance. Kelly and Nick have two sons.

Following in his parents footsteps, Kelly's oldest son, has joined the United States Navy and is now stationed in Great Lakes, Illinois for his basic training. After he has accomplished his training Nick Jr. will be attending A-School in Pensacola, Florida, he is pursuing a career as a Crypto Technician.

Kelly said that she has no regrets.

This last section in this book I dedicated to those veterans that have served their country well and now some are in the church-yard, some rest beneath the Sea; and when our time shall come and we are called to go, I pray that we will meet with those we knew so many years ago.

Kraft, Howard R.
World War One
129th Field Artillery
Battery "C"
England,
France, Germany
05/29/1918-05/03/1919

The following information was donated to me by Jean Lamping, wife of Veteran William Lamping featured in this book; she offered me her step-fathers military history so that it could be documented in the Liberty of Congress and always is available for family and friends.

Howard R. Kraft, was born 17 June 1897, in Waukegan, Illinois, Cook County, he enlisted in the US Army during World War One, on 29 May 1918. After his Basic Training at Jefferson Barracks, MO, Howard was assigned to Battery "C", 129th Field Artillery, 35th Division. Battery "C" was originally organized at Independence, Mo., and shortly after the declaration of war by our Country upon Germany "Battery C" was mustered into the Federal Service in that City on Sunday, 5 August 1917.

At that time Battery "C" was commanded by one Captain, two LT's and two 2nd LT's, and had a total of one hundred and thirty-six enlisted men.

Following is a little story that I would like to share with my readers, it is all about the true journey that the Veterans in Battery "C" experienced.

Independence, Missouri the home of a large majority of the eligible men for military service was in gala attire. The courthouse lawn and square immediately began to assume the appearance of real war times with guns and soldiers; the Armory being the quarters of the boys, was the scene of many brilliant occasions. Foot and gun drill was the order of the day and was anxiously watched by the admiring sweethearts, wives, mothers, fathers and friends until the evening of 26 September 1917 when orders came to move; the entire population of the city turned out en-masse to give the boys a rousing send-off as they marched to the awaiting train on their first lap of a long journey to the shell swept battle fields of France.

After two days travel through the states of Kansas and Oklahoma they arrived at Camp Doniphan, or Fort Still, Oklahoma in early morning. After a march to camp, tents were pitched and Army life had become a reality.

Shortly after arrival, three Captains' took command of the Battery. On 10 November 1917, work and drill kept all of the men busy and time did not hang very heavily. The Battalion's first war lesson began with the construction of modern battle trenches and gun emplacements near Signal Mountain.

About a month later on 24 January 1918 a banquet and get-together meeting was given by the Battery. Many distinguished visitors were present, among them Brigadier General Berry (and his aide Major Gale), LT. Col. Robert M. Danford, Majors Miles, Stayton and Wilson and Capt. Sermon. All the officers made interesting speeches full of advice, encouragement and suggestions and were highly appreciated and well received. The music for the occasion was furnished by the ladies of the Lawton Music Club.

Intensive training of mounted drills, regardless of the weather conditions, was scheduled for the Battery until 8 May 1918, when orders to prepare to move were received, and on 10 May entrained for Camp Mills, NY via the Frisco. Their first stop was Oklahoma City, OK. Then on to Springfield, Missouri, where a short stop was made. After a days riding they arrived in Pacific, Missouri, where they left the train for a short hike, then on to St. Louis arriving there about 6:00 PM. About 9:00 P.M. they entrained in modern Pullmans, on the Clover Leaf, and the next stop was Frankfort, Indiana and passing through Toledo and Cleveland, Ohio, and Buffalo, New York. In Buffalo they were served refreshments by the Red Cross. At Hoboken, New Jersey they were transferred to a ferry for Long Island and arrived at Camp Mills, 14 May 1918.

On 20 May they received sailing orders and marched to the Canard piers and embarked about 10:00 A.M. on the Saxonia (R.M.S.) and at 5:00 P.M., they began their long trip to France. On 23 May the troops anchored off Halifax, N.S. and had a good view of the ruins of that city caused by the recent explosion of war munitions, probably the worst of its kind during the war.

After 17 days on the ocean they anchored at Tilbury Docks, London, England, on the night of 4 June, 1918, and disembarked on the morning of 5 June 1918. They immediately entrained for Winchester, England, then to Southampton where they embarked for La Havre, France on the steamship Viper, one of the swiftest ships in the British service.

Here the real tension of the trip began to be felt, especially by the officers. The English Channel, through which they were passing, had been the scene of disaster to many troop ships. Floating mines of the enemy, together with her many recent submarine activities, had wrought havoc to many British ships.

They arrived safely at La Havre on the morning of 8 June 1918, where they remained for a couple of days, fraternizing with the "Tommie's," and on the night of 10 June entrained for Angers, France, arriving there on the 11th and then a short "hike" brought them to the ancient French village of Andard.

It was at Andard that they received their famous "French Seventy-fives", together with some horses. Being the first American troops in the section of France, they were accorded a royal welcome by the entire populace.

On 16 June 1918 the entire regiment marched to Brain, colors were blessed in a large cathedral, by Father Curtis L. Tiernan, regimental chaplain.

On 17 August 1918 they broke camp and marched to Guer, entrained for Saulzures, where they arrived on 20 August and after a three day rest they began their march into German Territory. "The historical Alsace-Lorraine country", crossing the Vosges Mountains, at the extreme summit of which is a large stone marker, erected by Germany designating the dividing line between France and Alsace-Lorraine; they arrived at Kruth, situated in a valley, between two mountains, on 24 August 1918. It being a strong pro-German town in Germany territory, their reception was not a very cordial one.

The batteries arrived Sunday morning about 4:30 and they immediately went into position, and prepared to go into action, but none too soon. The Germans began a terrified bombardment of gas, shrapnel and high explosives about nightfall, but they gave them shell for shell throughout the night, and with dawn the firing ceased. This was now near the town of Metlach.

Immediately across the valley was a splendid view of Robinson Hill, made famous by the stand of the Alpine Chaussers, better known as the "Blue Devils of France," in the latter part of 1914 and up to the "Battle of Meterzal" on 15 June 1915. (This battle was one of the most bitterly contested of the war and has been immortalized by one of the great artists of France). Here the French lost about 60,000 men.

On the evening of 6 September 1918, they marched to the village of Cloyvilliers, where they were billeted in barns and remained until 9 September, then started northward, and after a long, tiresome march, bivouacked in the early morning hours in woods near Nancy.

The rain came down in torrents and mud was shoe to mouth deep. After trudging many weary kilometers, they passed through the city of Nancy abut 2.00 a.m. The city of Nancy is one of the largest and best known cities of France, presenting a weird scene while they marched through its streets; not a light was shown and no one except a lone sentry in sight.

After leaving Nancy, at a high ridge road, they witnessed one of the greatest artillery duels the world has ever known; the horizon was lighted up as though it were an electrical display. It was the great St. Muriel drive. The Company moved into the Forest De Haye, directly in the rear of St. Mihiel, and was held in reserve with horse's harnessed and full equipment on carriages, ready at any minute to advance and take position in line should they be needed.

They again took up the march on 15 September 1918. This proved to be the longest and hardest of any of the hikes yet experienced.

The horses were dying from exhaustion and exposure; feed was scarce and the roads heavy. Carcasses of dead horses lined the roadside; the men, carrying full packs, were footsore, and weary, and were virtually living on iron rations, still with some words of cheer from our officers they kept on without a murmur, and finally arrived in another forest where they rested for two days and a night.

After more traveling on 21 September they halted in a shell torn field. In the afternoon, they moved about a kilometer forward and established echelon in a draw and remained until after the greatest American battle ever fought, "The Battle of Argonne Forest."

About noon, 21 September 1918, orders were received to have the firing batteries in readiness to move forward at any time, and about 5:00 p.m. they pulled out, to take up their position on Hill 290.

They proceeded up a shell swept, camouflaged road, past their ammunition dump, in rain, mud and darkness. Here they left the road and took out across a field with virtually no road and mud hub deep, the horses in bad shape, they arrived at their positions.

It was here that they experienced their first German barrage. Also the Germans were gassing heavily. The morning of 26 September, was to begin the great offensive along the entire front. Battery "C" was selected to accompany the infantry in their advance.

This was the greatest drive ever launched against the Hun and later proved to be his "Waterloo". Throughout the night of the 25th, and into the morning of the 26th the Hun kept pounding at them with guns of all calibers. At 1:00 a.m. of the 26th, the Allies began the great drive.

In a distance the horizon had the appearance of a severe electrical storm. Their guns were in action everywhere, the land is rolling here and it seemed as though the very hills opened up and commenced to belch fire and flame.

They kept a continuous barrage from 4:20 a.m. to 7:20 a.m., firing approximately 2,500 rounds of ammunition for the one battery. The guns of the enemy had been completely silenced by their artillery fire and immediately after they ceased firing and pulled their guns and prepared to advance to support their infantry who had already gone "over the top"; they were now in Boureuilles where their advance was stopped by the blowing up of bridges by the retreating enemy. Ahead to the left front they could see their infantry desperately charging up a slope and attacking the machine gun pits of the enemy. The German airplanes were trying to harass them, but were met by the Allied planes that were battling directly above.

On 27 September in a heavy rain they advanced to the woods and went into position northeast of Hill 239, moving again at 6 a.m. they went into position about 400 meters southeast of Hill 221, where they fired several barrages on Carpentry and Baulny. Here they remained throughout the night.

Early on the morning of the 28th, being previously selected to follow the infantry, they received orders to move to Charpentry to cover their advance.

Advancing they passed through Cheppy and on to Charpentry. Enroute they met captured batteries of German 77's, German machine gun nests with their own men piled high in front of them; men dead and dying lined the roadside, mutilated horses, destroyed guns, and material of all kinds, presented a scene that is impossible to describe.

They were now on the Route Nationate, here their advance was continually meeting stiff resistance by attacks from the enemy airplanes that would sweep down parallel with their column and turn loose volley after volley of machine gun fire. Here they suffered their first casualty in the death of Private Robert K. Mayfield. A shell passed through one of their fourgons, instantly killing Mayfield on the opposite side.

They were now moving into Charpentry; crossing a bridge spanning the Aisne River, they took cover in an old orchard near the ruins of this village, loaded their guns and immediately went into action.

The German trenches and dugouts here showed why they had held this line for four years. Their trenches were fortified with rock walls and their dugouts were in many instances 40 feet below the ground, with all the conveniences of home, electric lights, baths, kitchen, dining room and sleeping quarters, Some of their boys who had been on short rations for the past few days, in exploring the hastily abandoned quarters, found jam molasses, butter and course black bread, also some Belgian hares, which were doubtless being raised for the Hun officers mess, contributed to the feast enjoyed by them.

Allied tanks began streaming past us, coming from the front; then a squadron of cavalry was seen falling back; stragglers of the infantry passed and informed them that the Germans had broken the line and were coming over (which report proved to be incorrect) however, the Hun made three counterattacks all of which were repulsed.

After being relieved by the First Division on 4 October they retired to Signeulles, about 40 kilometers in the rear, for a few days of much needed rest. Arriving at Signeulles, many men were found to be unfit for immediate service and were left at field hospitals to recuperate while the remaining part of the battery took up the march again.

On 12 October, they left Signeulles, still raining as usual, and after an all night hike spent the day in a forest. In Rapt they spent a day, they were now moving into the Woevre sector of the world's famous Verdun front. The fighting in this sector had been dilatory for the past two years, the French having established and held their lines with the aid of their many forts. The enemy having been aroused by the activities along the entire line was making preparations for a big drive in the sector also, as the divisions of the Yanks began to pour in. They arrived in the forest near Ft. Rozellier, on the morning of 16 October.

On 9 November orders were to advance and support the 81st Division Infantry who were going over the top. At 11:00 a.m. they moved forward, Battery "C" of the First Battalion, and Batteries E and F of the Second Battalion. Arriving in position near Moulainville De Bosse, they were in an open field, looking across a marsh with a dense growth of underbrush, probably four feet high.

Their guns were laid in waiting on the early morning of the 10th, all this being done in darkness and the usual rain. The rain continued throughout the entire day, gradually getting worse as the day wore on. The heavy weather had prevented the enemy from getting range on them, although they kept up continual firing throughout the day and night. This weather continued throughout the morning of the 11th. At 9:00 a.m. they received orders to cease firing at 11:00 a.m. and were being advised of the signing of the armistice. However, they continued to fire until about 10:30 a.m., when the weather began to clear, the fog lifted and the enemy was starting to locate them with their large caliber guns. Shells began breaking all around with several hitting close shattering a wheel. All this time the enemy had been throwing a sweeping barrage.

At 11:00 a.m. the firing eased almost as suddenly as it had begun over four years before. A deep silence seemed to fall over the entire line. There were no wild demonstrations; no cheers; the seriousness of the war had been impressed too firmly upon the minds of the men to be thrown off in a few minutes.

To men in gun pits, with pieces ready for action and plenty of ammunition and the fighting spirit at "high tide" it was hard to realize that the last mission had been performed. By noon, the clouds had broken away. The sun began to shine for the first time in weeks. The afternoon was bright and crisp.

That night, the moon shone out in its entire splendor. "No Man's Land" that night was basking in the mellow moonlight instead of the flashings of the cannons that had held sway so long. It was a sight that will long remain in the minds of all who gazed across that expanse of country dividing the two lines that memorable night of 11 November 1918.

On the morning of the 12th, they were ordered to return to original positions; remaining here for a few days, then pulled their guns and returned to the echelon about two kilometers distant in the woods and hills, at Camp Claire Cote. Here time was taken up in the regular routine of fatigues and drills. Time soon began to hang heavily on their hands as the days wore on.

They were located in an isolated place, with nothing to divert our minds; no amusements of any sort; expecting any day or leave for somewhere (either Germany or home, but preferably home) and believing almost any rumor, but holding firmly to the ones which favored early return home.

Arriving at Camp Claire Cote, they found the billets, stables and surroundings in a deplorable condition. The billets were put in good shape; the stables were reconstructed and put in good condition; kitchen was enlarged and improved; and an old stable was thoroughly renovated.

On 21 January 1919, they began hiking out of the woods and hills, away from the shell-swept, battle-scarred fields of Northern France and after two days arrived at the small ancient French village of Culey.

Orders were out for an early move towards the coast; a sailing date has been booked, and each and every man believing he has "fought a good fight and kept the faith" and helped to make the world safe for democracy, hopes soon to be in the Land of the Free and the Home of the Brave, and to be welcomed by the mothers, wives, sweethearts, fathers and friends as never before; hoping that the black clouds of war may never again hang over our fair land.

Howard H. Kraft was honorably discharged from the Army 3 May 1919 at Great Camp, Illinois. For his military service he was awarded several Medals and Ribbons.

Brown, Earl Amos

United States Army	Medic, 338th Engineers
World War Two	Italy, Naples, Foggia & Rome,
Oran, Algeria	Oran, Algeria
01/06/1943-10/09/1945	Deceased February 1980

 Earl A. Brown was born on 29 July 1923, in Sedalia, a city in central Missouri, he grew up and attended schools there along with his Brother Clyde (a U.S. Marine), and his sister Georgia.

On 6 January 1943, at age nineteen years, Earl signed up for the United States Military, after filing an endless number of papers, he then took a written test; he passed that, next it was time for a physical. After passing his entire test, Earl was selected for the U.S. Army Engineers.

Earl was transported to Fort Leavenworth, Texas where he accomplished his basic training, he was attached to the 338th Engineers, he was a medic.

During World War Two, the 338th Engineer Regiment rebuilt the vital port of Northern Italy, in advance of the Fifth United States Army assault on the German positions in the Po Valley, Italy.

The Regiment departed New York on 28 April 1943 (likely on the SS Santa Rosa) and arrived in Oran, Algeria, on 12 May 1943. They landed in Italy on 8 February 1944.

The town of Livorno(Leghorn) NW Italy was in need as a supply base for the North Apennines (mountain system extending from NW Italy S to the Strait of Messina) campaign, but the port was the most thoroughly demolished one in the Mediterranean.

The Germans had created barricades, blown bridges, laid mines, and sunk twenty ships to completely seal off the harbor entrances. The Allies also contributed to the destruction; in some 50 raids during the first half of 1944, they dropped more than 1,000 tons of bombs.

Elements of the 34th Infantry Division (U.S.) had captured Livorno on 19 July 1944. The 338th Engineers, which had been working on hospitals in Rome, had no experience in port repair, but drew the assignment anyway.

Twelve men from the 338th Engineers arrived in the city a few hours later to clear mines from predetermined routes into the port area. Leghorn was heavily mined, and for the first few days little other than mine clearing could be accomplished. As the mine-clearing teams made room, more elements of the 338th arrived, set up quarters, and began preparing a berth for the LST and the LCT carrying construction equipment.

The primary task for the 338th Engineer was to reconstruct berths and ships. Within a month, berths for six Liberty ships had been completed giving Leghorn a capacity of 5,000 tons per day.

As the berths were completed, the 338th turned its attention to rebuilding roads, bridges, hospitals, depots, and camps. Working together with Italian soldiers and civilians, the engineers were able to amass and distribute the large volume of supplies required.

On 9 October 1945, after the surrender of Japan, Earl was honorably discharged and was awarded the Good Conduct Medal, European-African-Middle Eastern Campaign Medal with 2 bronze service stars, World War II Victory Medal, Honorable Service Lapel Button WWII, Marksman Badge with Rifle Bar and several ribbons.

Also for its accomplishments, the 338th Engineers were awarded the Meritorious Service Unit Plaque per General Orders No66, Headquarters, Peninsular Base Section on 24 February 1945.

Earl Brown returned to civilian life and resumed his place in the working field by opening his own business (Women's Apparel). In 1952 he married Delores (Dee) Brown and they had three sons.

Veteran Earl A. Brown died on 3 February 1980; his wife Delores (Dee) is a resident of Levittown, Pennsylvania and keeps busy with gardening, sewing and crafts. I learned about Earl from my daughter Renee, one of her best friends (Terry) is the son of Earl Brown. And I thank you Mrs. Brown for being able to furnish her your late husband's military information, and I'm proud to include it in this book in recognition of his contribution to our American Freedom.

The 16TH Infantry Regiment—is a regiment of the United States Army. The 34th Infantry Regiment and 11th Infantry Regiment consolidated into the 16th Infantry Regiment on 3 March 1869. The 11th Infantry's history prior to the consolidation is normally included with the 16th's. The Regiment took part in some of the hardest-fought battles of the war.

Infantry—is a branch of the Army who fight on foot, soldiers specifically trained to engage fight and defeat the enemy in face-to-face combat; infantry thus bear the brunt of warfare, and suffer the greatest number of causalities.

The next Veteran you will read about was killed in Germany during World War Two.

Alfred Schneider
United States Army
World War Two
Reconnaissance Battalion
Died in Battle, April 1945 in Germany

Private Alfred Schneider, top left corner, World War Two Soldier entered the Army in September 1943, he was the oldest of the seven brothers that served in the United States Military during World War Two, (their were 16 children total) Alfred lost his life on 21 April 1945 while fighting with a Reconnaissance Battalion in Germany, he was 30 years old.

Following his death, his wife Frances received the Silver Star for Alfred's heroic courage and actions on behalf of a wounded comrade, which resulted in his death in Germany.

The letter addressed to the family of Private Alfred Schneider was as follows,

"For gallantry in action against the enemy on 21 April 1945, the motorized reconnaissance party of which Private Schneider was a member encountered an enemy force and, in an exchange of fire, the gunner of the vehicle was wounded.

Private Schneider promptly removed the wounded soldier to a place of comparative safety where he administered first aid. Choosing to protect the casualty from capture or further injury, he remained at his side, but by doing so was compelled to engage the enemy force in another exchange of fire, in which he was killed."

Alfred Schneider's other six brothers were Arthur and Roland, both entered the Army in March, 1941. Arthur was discharged July 1945 after serving in the Southwest Pacific. Roland who also served in the Southwest Pacific was discharged October 1945. James, after serving with the Military Police was released in the fall of 1944. Norman served two and one-half years in the Army; he was discharged in September 1945. Arnold a gunner's mate 3/c served in the US Navy since 1943 and Clarence was a Soldier in the United States Army.

Alfred Schneider is the father of Jean Lamping, she had lost her father while just a young tot and we are proud to be able to document his passing for future military history. Jean also was able to donate the photo of the seven brothers featured on the cover of this book. Jean's husband William is also a veteran along with his two brothers that are all featured in this book.

Anthony, Charles B. (Tony), CPL.
United States Army   World War Two
                       Korea, and Vietnam
Deceased June, 2002
03/07/1945-10/01/1966

Born 30 May 1929 to Charles and Marie Anthony in Montgomery, W. Virginia, Charles had two sisters, Julia Mode and Carmella. While Charles attended schools in Montgomery, he was on the Varsity Football team, Tech #47. During the summertime when he was about twelve or thirteen, Charles worked in the coal mines; he also was a shoe repairmen's helper around his fathers "Shoe Shop" in Smithers, W.V., until he was old enough to sign up for the United States Army.

Charles entered into the military March 1945; after passing his physical and written exams, he was transferred to an Army base for his basic and combat training.

During World War Two, Charles was attached to Headquarters Company 16th Infantry Regiment, 1st Division. He was assigned Occupational Specialist Medium Tank Crewman; like I mentioned earlier in the book, the Infantry men are the ground troops, they are the foot soldiers, and they are trained to defeat the enemy. While Charles was serving in the European Theatre of War he also prepared meals for the troops. Charles served in France and Germany until the surrender of the Germans.

For his military service he was awarded the Good Conduct Medal, European Service Medal, WW II Victory Medal, Army Occupation Medal, National Defense Medal among others.

After returning to America he was recommended for further military training, he was sent to Fort Meade, Maryland and trained with the Armored Command Basic Training.

When the Korean War broke out Charles was recalled to overseas duty, this time he was stationed in Japan, while serving in Japan Charles continued his schooling at the Seventh U.S.A. Noncommissioned Officers Academy, graduating as a Corporal (non-commissioned-officer) with Company "A", 8th Engineer Battalion, 24 April 1959. Along with his rating he also was awarded several medals after the Korean Occupation, he earned his 2nd Good Conduct Medal, Korean Service Medal, National Defense Service Medal and several Ribbons.

After returning back to the United States from Japan, Charles was stationed at Ft. Campbell, KY with the 511th Engineer Company, where he continued learning; he also did a stint in Paris, France.

In February 1964 while serving at Fort Dix, New Jersey, Charles was getting his mustering out papers, including his DD-214, along with more medals. Then he was informed that his military career would be extended until 1 October 1966 because of the Vietnam War.

In 1966 Charles was honorably discharge from the U.S. Military and was awarded more medals, some that Charles received were Republic of Korea Presidential Unit Citation Badge, Honorable Service Lapel Button WW II, his 3rd Good Conduct Medal, Marksman Badge w/Rifle & Carbine Bars, Bronze Clasp w/4 loops, the Silver Service Star w/Oak Leaf Cluster in lieu of five (5) bronze Service Stars.

After Charles military service he worked at his father's Shoe Repair Shop, and then he worked at Imperial Chemical Industries, a position he held for twenty-five years, retiring in 1991.

Over the years Charles held memberships in several organizations, participating as President of the United Steel Workers of America Local 12886, from 1987-1989, President of the Lion's Club, 1992-1994, in Middletown, Delaware, Knights of Columbus Council #6624, and St. Joseph Catholic Church, Middletown, Delaware, he was a 4th degree.

After retiring Charles and his wife Anna bought a small farm in Townsend, Delaware and with their two children, Val & Rickie, they went into raising pigs for about seven or eight years. In 1995 they moved to St. Cloud, Florida.

Although Charles was retired, he still worked at Wal-Mart part-time as a greeter, in St. Cloud, Florida from, 1995-1999. He is the father of two children, a daughter, Valerie, his son Rickie, Rickie was also a retired military veteran that had served for 20 years in the United States Air Force and now works as mechanic at Dover Air Force Base, Delaware. Charles Sr. has five grandchildren and four great-grandchildren. Veteran Cpl. Charles B. Anthony (Tony) passed on 9 June 2002. This military information was donated by Charles Anthony's widow.

Cicero G. (Lucky) Harwell, Sr. Master Sgt.
United States Air Force
July 1948-1970
Deceased October 2005

Also featured in this book is Elizabeth Harwell, wife of the above deceased veteran, Lucky met Elizabeth (Betty) Weldon while they were both serving in the U.S.A.F., she was a typist and he was a typing instructor. Lucky was later changed to the Personnel Field, which he stayed in until 1967, when he retained as a Loadmaster on C-124 and later on C-130 Aircraft. Lucky was discharged in July 1952; he remained in the Air Force Reserves. In 1954 Lucky was recalled to active duty and made it his career until 1970.

After he was recalled, his wife Betty traveled to different bases with her husband. During his re-enlistment Lucky was stationed in Colorado Springs, Moriyanna Air Station, Nagoya, Japan, Hickam Air Force Base, Honolulu, Hawaii, Bolling AFB, Washington, DC, Orlando AFB, FL, San Antonio, TX, and Ramstein Air Base, Germany, his wife Betty traveled with him always. He retired as Senior Master Sergeant. Lucky Harwell passed away in 2005.

Lucky Harwell was from Camden, AR., where his parents had a eighty-three acre farm, he enlisted into the Air Force in July 1948.

APPENDIX

Amelia Earhart. 1897-1937

Amelia Earhart was born on 24 July 1897 in Atchison, Kansas. Her flying career began in Los Angeles in 1921 when, at age 24 she took flying lessons from Neta Snook and bought her first airplane.

In July 1936 she took delivery of a Lockheed 10E "Electra", financed by Purdue University, and started planning her round-the-world flight. Noonan, a former Pan Am pilot, would be Earhart's navigator and sole companion in flight for the entire trip. They departed in Miami on 1 June, they arrived at Lie, New Guinea on 29 June. About 22,000 miles of the journey had been completed. The remaining 7,000 miles would all be over the Pacific Ocean.

On 2 July, 1937 at 0000 GMT, Earhart and Noonan took off from Lae. Their last positive position reports and sighting were over the Nukumanu Islands, about 800 miles into the flight. After six hours of frustrating attempts at two-way communications, contact was lost.

A coordinated search by the Navy and Coast Guard was organized and no physical evidence of the flyers or their plane was ever found. There are many theories, the latest theory is written in a book titled; "The Truth at Last", by Mike Campbell.

Civilian Conservation Corps—from Wikipedia

The Civilian Conservation Corps (CCC) was public relief program that operated from 1933 to 1942 in the United States for unemployed, unmarried men from relief families, ages 18-25, Robert Fechner was the head of the agency.

A part of the New Deal of President Franklin D. Roosevelt, who provided unskilled manual labor jobs related to the conservation and development of natural resources in rural lands owned by federal, state and local governments. The CCC was designed to provide jobs for young men, to relieve families who had difficulty finding jobs during the Great Depression in the United States while at the same time implementing a general natural resource conservation program in every state and territory. Maximum enrollment at any one time was 300,000; in nine years 3 million young men participated in the CCC, which provided them with shelter, clothing, and food, together with a small wage of $30 a month ($25 of which had to be sent home to their families).

During the time of the CCC, volunteers planted nearly 3 billion trees to help reforest America, constructed more than 800 parks nationwide and upgraded most state parks, updated forest fire fighting methods, and built a network of service buildings and public roadways in remote areas. Despite its popular support, the CCC was never a permanent agency; it depended on emergency and temporary Congressional legislation for its existence. By 1942, with World War II and the draft in operation, need for work relief declined and Congress voted to close the program.

Navy Seabees in Marine Uniforms-Often we see in pictures a U.S. Navy Seabee in a U.S. Marine uniform. The reason for this is that during World War One, it didn't take long before the Germans and Japanese learned that the U.S. Navy had a special unit of the branch that were trained in construction skills, put in Marine uniforms and trained for combat also. They were the U.S. Navy Seabees (Construction Battalions).

These are some of the men who came ashore or in-country directly with the invasion troops and unloaded ships and to build the infrastructure needed for sustained operations against the enemy. The Germans and the

Japanese were wise to the fact that the Seabees ware different uniform, and killed them first, until later when the military issued them Marine uniforms to be worn when going in with the Marines on invasions.

POM/MPOM-Procurer of Material Motor Pool Occupation Vehicles. **fact**—Standard Oil Company of New Jersey was given the contract to supply the design and oil for fuel facilities for Iceland and other bases in Scotland and Ireland during World War Two. **the pontoon**—Nick-named the "Magic Box", back in 1940 Captain Laycock, CEC, USN began to consider the difficulties of transporting cargo from ship to shore, and of a quick establishment of unloading facilities where nothing existed before.

He conceived the idea of a steel pontoon which would overcome these problems.

For molds, his desk was covered with cigar boxes which he fastened together in a myriad of ways until he evolved the pontoon structures which the Navy used so successfully in its landings in Africa, Salerno, on the Normandy Coast, Guadalcanal and hundreds of other Islands in the South and Central and Western Pacific.

At military funerals the flag that is draped over the coffin is surrendered to the veteran's widow. **our Flag**—Have you ever noticed the honor guard pays meticulous attention to correctly folding the United States of America Flag 13 times? You probable thought it was to symbolize the original 13 colonies, but we learn something new every day.

The 1st fold of the flag is a symbol of life.

The 2nd fold is a symbol of the belief in eternal life

The 3rd fold is made in honor and remembrance of the veterans departing the ranks who gave a portion of their lives for the defense of the country to attain peace throughout the world.

The 4th fold represents the weaker nature, for as American citizens trusting in God, it is Him we turn to in times of peace as well as in time of war for His divine guidance.

The 5th fold is a tribute to the country, for in the words of Stephen Decatur, "Our Country, in dealing with other countries, may she always be right; but it is still our country, right or wrong".

The 6th fold is for where people's hearts lie. It is with their heart that they pledge allegiance to the flag of the United States of America, and the Republic for which it stands, one Nation under God, indivisible, with Liberty and Justice for all.

The 7th fold is a tribute to its Armed Forces, for it is through the Armed Forces that they protect their country and their flag against all her enemies, whether they be found within or without the boundaries of their republic.

The 8th fold is a tribute to the one who entered into the valley of the shadow of death, that we might see the light of day.

The 9th fold is a tribute to womanhood, and Mothers. For it has been through their faith, their love, loyalty and devotion that the character of the men and women who have made this country great has been molded.

The 10th fold is a tribute to the father, for he, too, has given his sons and daughters for the defense of their country since they were first born.

The 11th fold represents the lower portion of the seal of King David and King Solomon and glorifies in the Hebrews eyes, the God of Abraham, Isaac and Jacob.

The 12th fold represents an emblem of enternity and glorifies, in the Christians eyes, God the Father, the Son and Holy Spirit.

The 13th fold, or when the flag is completely folded, the stars are uppermost reminding them of their nation's motto, "In God We Trust".

After the flag is completely folded and tucked in, it takes on the appearance of a cocked hat, ever reminding us of the soldiers who served under General George Washington, and the Sailors and Marines who served under Captain John Paul Jones, who were followed by their comrades and shipmates in the Armed Forces of the United States, preserving for them the rights, privileges and freedoms they enjoy today.

At military funerals, the 21-gun salute stands for the sum of the numbers in the year 1776?

There are some traditions and ways of doing things that have deep meaning. In the future, you'll see flags folded and now you will know why.

ACKNOWLEDGEMENTS

The pictures on the cover of this book were donated by:

Top left,	Donald R. Smith CWO4, featured in this book
Top right,	Kelly Kern, featured in the book
Center Photo,	Donated by: William Bottorff (fifth on the right)
Bottom left,	by my son, William the Artist
Bottom right,	End of the war, unconditional surrender, by: Vincent Parzyck

ABOUT THE AUTHOR

The author, Irene J. Dumas was born and raised in Trenton, New Jersey, and lived in Moorestown, NJ. Following her retirement from the NJ Department of Environmental Protection, she moved to Waverly, Florida in the summer of 2004. She was impressed by the brave and selfless service of many of the veterans she had met as well as their spirit and zest for life. She wrote a small book in 2003 about their exploits, followed by *A Salute to Our Veterans—Vignettes of Those Who Made the Difference (1939-2000)* in 2005. That book was so well received she was encouraged to write this book.